CHARLES BA

THE FLOWEI

ns
CHARLES BAUDELAIRE

THE FLOWERS OF EVIL

Translated from the French
by
John E. Tidball

BISHOPSTON EDITIONS

First published in French 1868

This translation first published 2021

Copyright © 2021 by John E. Tidball

All rights reserved

ISBN 9798701610796

CONTENTS

Page 7 — Translator's Note

Page 11 — Epigraph

Page 13 — To the Reader

Page 15 — Spleen and the Ideal

Page 145 — Parisian Scenes

Page 177 — Wine

Page 185 — Flowers of Evil

Page 213 — Revolt

Page 223 — Death

Page 237 — Other Poems

Page 247 — Alphabetical Index

Translator's Note

Most of the original poems in this book were published by Baudelaire in 1857 and 1861 under the title *Les Fleurs du Mal (The Flowers of Evil)*. Contrary to popular belief *Les Fleurs du Mal* was not initially conceived by Baudelaire as a cycle of poems like, for example, Tennyson's *Maud* or Housman's *A Shropshire Lad*. Indeed, the poems were written throughout the poet's lifetime and were only selected later for inclusion in *Les Fleurs*. Moreover, the order of poems differs considerably between the editions of 1857 and 1861, although there does appear to be a kind of "secret architecture", especially in the 1861 edition which contained several new poems but lacked the six pieces which had been censored by the court when Baudelaire and his editor were prosecuted in 1857 for offending against public morals.

Baudelaire died in 1867, and in 1868 some of his friends published a posthumous edition of *Les Fleurs du Mal*, which contained most of Baudelaire's other poems, some of which he would almost certainly not have wished to include himself. For the purposes of the present work the poems are presented as a new collection rather than as a cycle, because I have included all of the posthumously published pieces, as well as the six poems that were banned in 1857. Interestingly, it was not until 1949 that the judgment was overturned and their publication in France was authorised. The poems in question are *Lesbos, To Her who is too Gay, The Lethe, The Jewels, Damned Women (Delphine and Hippolyta)* and *The Metamorphoses of the Vampire*.

Also published posthumously in 1869 was a collection entitled *Petits poèmes en prose (Little Prose Poems)*, now more commonly known as *Le Spleen de Paris (Paris Spleen)*. An epilogue in verse, which was added to that collection by the editors at the time, has here been included as an epilogue to the section *Parisian Scenes*. To the best of my knowledge, it has not appeared in any previous edition of *The Flowers of Evil*. Finally, as an appendix to the main work, I have added several poems that were not included in any of the three original editions.

— John E. Tidball, January 2021

DEDICATION

To the impeccable poet
To the perfect magician of French letters
To my very dear and very revered
Master and friend
Théophile Gautier
With sentiments
Of the most profound humility
I dedicate
These sickly flowers
C.B.

EPIGRAPH FOR A CONDEMNED BOOK

Dear reader, peaceful and bucolic,
Upstanding, sober and benign,
Discard this book that's saturnine,
Libidinous and melancholic.

If you've not done your rhetoric
With Satan, that most artful dean,
Discard! there's nothing you could glean,
Or you might think me an hysteric.

But if, resisting its allure,
Your eye can fathom the abyss,
Read me, and learn to love me more,

Poor suffering soul in search of bliss,
Your paradise, your promised land,
Have pity on me! ... or be damned!

TO THE READER

Stupidity, error, parsimony, and vice
Consume our consciousness, and waste our body's force,
And we are wont to feed our affable remorse
Like beggars who provide nutrition for their lice.

Our sins are obstinate, and our repentance faint,
And when we do confess, we want a hefty fee,
And gaily we return to our debauchery,
Believing by false tears to wash away our taint.

Upon his evil pillow, Satan Trismegist
Lulls us and casts his spell on our enchanted mind,
And the rich metal of our will is thus resigned
To being vaporised by this skilled alchemist.

The Devil pulls the strings by which our deeds are swayed,
And things that are repugnant hold us in their spell.
Each day we take a further step down into Hell,
Serenely passing through the putrid, stinking shade.

Just as an impecunious rake will bite and kiss
The old, tormented breast of some senescent whore,
We steal, along the way, forbidden fruits, before
Squeezing their dried-up flesh in search of hidden bliss.

Like maggots tightly packed and swarming in our brain,
A horde of Demons feast and belch their fetid breath,
And, when we breathe, an unperceived river of Death
Flows silently through every artery and vein.

If rape, malignancy, inferno, or the blade,
Have not embroidered yet, with their designs ornate,
The banal canvas of our pitiable fate,
It is, alas! because our soul is too afraid.

But in among the jackals, panthers, apes, and hounds,
The scorpions, the vultures, reptiles, snakes, and all
The yelping, growling beasts that leap and creep and crawl
Around the zoo of vice with which our life abounds,

There's one that is more hideous, more loathsome still!
He does not make grand gestures, nor shout noisily,
Yet he would gladly turn the earth into debris,
And in a yawn would swallow up the world at will.

He is Ennui! He dreams of rack and guillotine,
Smoking his hookah pipe, his eye moist with a tear.
You know him, reader, this delicate monster here,
— Duplicitous reader, — my fellow man, — my kin!

SPLEEN AND THE IDEAL

I. — BENEDICTION

When, by decree of the supreme authority,
The Poet is brought forth into this dismal sphere,
His mother, in her dread, and full of blasphemy,
Raises her fists to God, who takes pity on her:

— "Ah! would that I had spawned a writhing viper's nest,
Instead of giving suck to this absurd vexation!
Accursèd be the night when at delight's behest
My womb conceived the dawning of my expiation.

Since of all women on this earth you've chosen me
To be my wretched husband's odium and shame,
And since I cannot cast this dire monstrosity
Like an unwelcome billet-doux into the flame,

I shall inflict this hatred, which has taken root,
Upon the instrument of your malignity,
And it shall not give forth one single fetid shoot,
So tightly shall I twist this miserable tree!"

Thus does she swallow down the vile froth of her ire,
And being ignorant of plans that are sublime,
In the depths of Gehenna starts to build the pyre
On which is consummated all maternal crime.

However, through an unseen Angel's ministry,
The outcast Child grows strong, and thrives beneath the sun,
And everything he eats and drinks appears to be
As nectar and ambrosia blended into one.

He frolics with the wind, he talks with clouds, and keeps
Himself inspired by singing of the Pilgrim's Way.
And the kind Spirit, following his progress, weeps
To see him happy as a woodland bird at play.

All those whom he would love observe him with unease,
Or, being emboldened by his serenity,
Compete to see who best can make him ill at ease,
And test him with their spite and animosity.

Into the bread and wine prepared for him to sup
They add a filthy mix of saliva and ash.
In their hypocrisy, they shun all he might touch,
Accusing one another of treading in his tracks.

His wife goes out in public, crying vulgarly:
"Since he finds me so fair and worthy to adore,
I'll cast myself as some Hellenic deity,
And be adorned with gold made from the finest ore.

And I'll indulge myself with incense, nard, and myrrh,
With genuflexions, tender meats, and heady wine,
To see if, in a heart that loves me, I can stir
The homage due to God, obeisance divine!

And then, when I grow tired of this impious play,
My hands, dainty yet strong, will exercise their art.
And my nails, like a harpy's nails, will carve a way
Into the very confines of his foolish heart.

And, like a fledgling bird that quivers in the nest,
To satisfy the hunger of my favourite hound,
I'll tear that bleeding heart, still beating, from his breast,
And cast it with disdain before him on the ground!"

Upward to Heaven, where he sees a splendid throne,
Serene, the Poet lifts his arms in piety,
And the bright beacon, from his lucid spirit flown,
Obscures from him the sight of man's ferocity:

"Praise be to you, O God, who grant us suffering
As remedy divine for our impurity,
The best and purest essence that will surely bring
Your succour to the strong, your holy ecstasy!

I know that for the Poet you have kept a place
Among the happy ranks of holy Seraphim,
And that unto the heavenly eternal feast
Of Thrones, Dominions and Virtues summoned him.

I know that pain has a nobility unique,
That neither earth nor hell can ever undermine,
And that to fashion me a crown of pure mystique,
You must impose the laws of universe and time.

But neither the lost gems of ancient Palmyra,
Nor metals rare, nor pearls from the depths of the sea,
Assembled by your hand, can be one iota
Of this pure diadem, this crown you offer me.

For it shall be made only of the purest light,
Drawn from the sacred source of Heaven's primal rays,
And of which mortal eyes, however keen their sight,
Are only mirrors clouded by a mournful haze!"

II. — THE ALBATROSS

Often, to pass the time, seafarers will ensnare
An albatross, that giant bird whose great wings sweep
In carefree indolence a passage through the air,
Behind the ship that glides upon the bitter deep.

No sooner have they been set down upon the boards
Than these kings of the blue, now clumsy and forlorn,
Let their enormous wings, like useless trailing oars,
Pathetically drag beside their graceless form.

This once proud voyager has now become a freak!
Erstwhile so elegant, now mocked and travestied!
One of them, with a pipe, callously prods its beak;
Another stoops to ape the limping invalid!

The poet is akin to this prince of the clouds
Who haunts the raging storm and laughs at bows and slings.
In exile on the earth amid the baying crowds,
His movement is restricted by his giant wings.

III. — ELEVATION

Above the mountains, valleys, forests, lakes and meres,
Above the louring clouds, beyond the sun's bright face,
Beyond the compass of the far-flung realms of space,
Beyond the confines of the distant starry spheres,

My spirit, you go forth with great agility
And, like an able swimmer gliding through the sea,
You joyfully traverse the deep immensity
With an ineffable male sensuality.

Far from these fetid vapours you must soar and fly,
To seek purification in the higher air,
Imbibing, like a pure, ethereal liqueur,
The clear flame that inhabits the transparent sky.

Beyond the wearisome and all-consuming spleen
That weighs us down and clouds our lives with suffering,
Happy is he who can, upon a sturdy wing,
Take flight toward new pastures filled with light serene;

Whose lofty, noble thoughts, like skylarks on the wing,
Soar up into the sky upon a gentle breeze,
 — Who hovers over life, and understands with ease
The language of the flowers and every silent thing!

IV. — CORRESPONDENCES

Nature is a temple, where living colonnades
May sometimes utter words in which confusion lies.
Man wanders through its forests, where symbolic eyes
Observe him knowingly with their familiar gaze.

Like long, resounding echoes from the far beyond
That merge into a deep, tenebrous unity,
Immense as night and vast as daylight's clarity,
All colours, fragrances and accents correspond.

Some perfumes are as pure and cool as infants' flesh,
Soft as the oboe's sound, as meadows green and fresh,
— And others, rich, corrupt, triumphant, dissolute,

With the expansive range of all things infinite,
Like amber resin, musk, benzoin, and frankincense,
That sing euphoric hymns to spirit, mind, and sense.

V.

I love to contemplate those naked days of old,
When Phoebus would adorn his statues with fine gold.
When men and women, vigorous and indiscreet,
Enjoyed the fruits of love without fear or deceit,
And as the sun caressed their bodies, firm and sleek,
Took pleasure in the health of their noble physique.
And Cybele, fertile in gifts most generous,
In no way saw her progeny as onerous,
But, like a she-wolf with a bosom full of love,
Gave suckle to mankind with nectar from above.
Man, elegant, robust, and strong, was proud to sing
The praises of the beauties who proclaimed him king,
Unblemished fruits, devoid of taint, free to invite,
With flesh so smooth and firm, the ardent lover's bite!

The Poet of today, when he would contemplate
Those native splendours all arrayed in natural state,
The nakedness of men, and that of women, will,
Enveloping his soul, discern a sombre chill
Before this dreadful tableau, which he truly loathes,
Of monstrous apparitions crying out for clothes!
O piteous twisted forms! ridiculous physiques!
Torsos worthy of masks! skinny, pot-bellied, weak,
That some expedient god, implacable, alas,
As infants had wrapped up in swaddling clothes of brass!
And you, women, alas! of wan and sallow hue,
On whom indulgence feeds, and younger women too,
Who of maternal vice bear the heredity
And all the dreadful horrors of fecundity!

We have, in our corrupted nations, it is true,
Some beauties that the ancient peoples never knew:
Sad faces, gnawed and gnarled by ulcers of the heart,
And beauty, one might say, that languor can impart.

But those inventions of our poor retarded muse
Will never cause these ailing cultures to refuse
To their most noble youth their homage to avow,
— Exalted youth, of simple air and gentle brow,
Of limpid eye like water flowing pure and clear,
Dispersing far and wide, serene, without a care,
Like skies of azure blue, the flowers and the birds,
Its perfume and its warmth, its music and its words.

VI. — THE BEACONS

Rubens, calm Lethe's flow, garden of lethargy,
Pillow of youthful flesh where there can be no love,
But where life rushes in with such activity,
Like wave on ocean wave, and wind on wind above.

Da Vinci, mirror dark, tenebrous and profound,
Where charming angels wear a subtle, gentle smile,
Beneath the lofty pines and glaciers that surround
The enigmatic confines of their pleasant isle.

Rembrandt, sad hospital replete with murmurings,
Whose sole adornment is a massive crucifix,
Where tearful prayers arise out of putrescent things,
A shaft of winter light sharply traversing it.

And Michelangelo, where we see Hercules
Intermingled with Christs, surrounded by white clouds,
With powerful phantoms rising up out of Hades,
Their outstretched talons tearing at their winding shrouds.

The boxer's angry stance, the ostentatious faun,
You who could even see some beauty in a brute,
Great heart puffed up with pride, man feeble and forlorn,
Puget, the brooding emperor of the dissolute.

Watteau, bright carnival where many famous hearts,
Like flaming butterflies, flit gaily here and there,
Cool decors, chandeliers, which their soft light impart
Upon the dancers swirling to a charming air.

Goya, nightmarish scenes of things unspeakable,
Where foetuses are cooked in diabolic rites,
Hags with their looking-glass, nude girls, adorable,
Adjusting silken hose to tempt demonic sprites.

Delacroix, lake of blood where evil angels dwell,
Shaded by verdant pines in forests evergreen,
Where under brooding skies strange fanfares softly swell,
Like stifled sighs of Weber, gentle and serene.

These maledictions, blasphemies, and loud laments,
These ecstasies, these cries, these tears, these *Te Deum*,
Are like an echo from a thousand labyrinths.
It is, for mortal hearts, a heavenly opium!

It is a cry sent by a thousand sentinels,
An order broadcast by a thousand megaphones.
It is a beacon on a thousand citadels,
A hunting-horn that that calls for help in plaintive tones!

For truly, Lord, it is the homage most sublime
That we could ever pay to human dignity,
This ardent sob that rolls across the sands of time,
Expiring at the edge of your eternity!

VII. — THE SICK MUSE

O my poor muse, alas! what ails you so today?
Your hollow eyes betray dark thoughts and, each in turn,
I see reflected in your aspect the dismay
Of horror and delusion, cold and taciturn.

The green-hued succubus and the pink-tinted troll,
Did they pour you both fear and longing from their urns?
And did the nightmare grasp you in a vicious hold
And drown you deep inside a fabulous Minturnes?

I would that, redolent with odours of good health,
Your breast might ever be frequented by a wealth
Of noble thoughts, and that your blood might ever flow

With rhythmic sounds of songs and lays from long ago,
Where each in turn reign Phoebus, sire of melody,
And Pan, the lord of harvests in antiquity.

VIII. — THE VENAL MUSE

Muse of my heart, of ornate palaces so fond,
Will you, when January brings the rain and sleet,
The dreary snowbound days, the nights of dark despond,
Still have some embers that can warm your purple feet?

Will you be able to revive your marbled skin
With the nocturnal rays that penetrate your room?
Your palate dry, your purse with not a penny in,
Will you still reap some gold out of the vaults of gloom?

You'll need, for daily bread, to earn some recompense
And, like an altar boy, to swing the frankincense,
And sing some *Te Deum* in which you don't believe,

Or, like a starving dancer, let your charms appear
With laughter that is mingled with an unseen tear,
The boredom of the common rabble to relieve.

IX. — THE BAD MONK

Cloisters, in former times, displayed on their high walls
Scenes from the Sacred Truth of which the Scriptures told,
That lent an air of warmth to those exalted halls,
Which otherwise would be too austere and too cold.

In times when Christian faith grew stronger every day,
More than one famous monk, now lost to memory,
Would make the burial ground his artist's atelier,
Where he would honour Death with great simplicity.

— My soul's a vaulted tomb which I, bad cenobite,
Inhabit as I wander in eternal night.
Nothing adorns this cloister that I so despise.

O good-for-nothing monk! When shall I ever find,
Within the living drama of my wretched mind,
The labour of my hands and the love of my eyes?

X. — THE ENEMY

My youth was filled with days of dark and stormy skies,
Occasionally lit by shafts of brilliant sun.
So violent were the storms, that now my garden lies
Devoid of all its fruits of ripe vermilion.

And now that I have touched the autumn of my thoughts,
I must employ the hoe, the rake, the fork and spade,
So that the flooded land is rid of all its faults,
Where torrents gouged great holes as deep as any grave.

But who knows if the flowers my dreams now see in bud
Will find within this soil, diluted by the flood,
The mystic nourishment that they will need to thrive?

— O Torment! Anguish! Pain! Cruel Time devours our life,
And this dark Enemy that gnaws us deep inside
With the blood that we lose grows and is fortified!

XI. — THE RANSOM

To pay his ransom man must toil
In two fields of volcanic rock,
Which he must harrow to unlock
The underlying fertile soil.

To cultivate a slender stem,
Or extricate some meagre ears
Of corn, he must, with salty tears,
Perpetually water them.

One field is Art, the other Love.
— To make the verdict more benign
When the authority divine
Dispenses justice from above,

He must have granaries abrim
With harvests of abundant grain,
And blooms whose shapes and colours gain
Approval from the Seraphim.

XII. — THE JINX

Such a great burden to support
Would, Sisyphus, require your grit!
One's heart may well be up to it,
But Art is long, and Time is short.

Far from the famous cemeteries,
Toward a lonely catacomb,
My sad heart, like a muffled drum,
Goes beating plaintive monodies.

— Many a gem lies buried still,
Far from the pickaxe and the drill,
In darkness, far beneath the ground.

Many a flower gives with regret
Its sweet perfume, like a secret,
In solitude vast and profound.

XIII. — THE FORMER LIFE

Long did I dwell beneath enormous colonnades
Upon which ocean suns cast myriad shafts of light,
And whose great pillars stood majestic in the night,
Resembling the huge columns of basaltic caves.

The billows, surging with reflections of the skies,
With echoes of a solemn, mystic harmony,
Mingled the powerful chords of their rich symphony
With colours of the sunset, mirrored in my eyes.

And there I spent my days in hedonistic calm,
Beneath the splendour of the azure firmament,
And there were naked slaves, with odours redolent,

Who would refresh my brow with fronds of waving palm,
Whose one and only duty was to penetrate
The dolorous enigma of my languid state.

XIV. — VERY FAR FROM HERE

Here is the sacred dwelling-place
Where this young woman, full of grace,
Lies decked with gems and finest lace.

Her fingers gently fan her breast,
Her elbows into cushions pressed,
While weeping ponds attend her rest.

This is the room of Dorothy.
— And in the distance pond and breeze
Are sobbing their sweet melodies
To rock this spoilt child tenderly.

From head to toe, prepared to please,
Her skin is brushed exquisitely
With fragrant oils and potpourris.
— And flowers swoon in ecstasy.

XV. — TRAVELLING GYPSIES

The prophet tribe, those seers of incandescent eye,
Bearing their progeny, took to the road last night,
The women satisfying eager appetites
From hanging breasts, wherein their ample treasures lie.

The menfolk are on foot, with weaponry that gleams,
Walking beside the wagons sheltering their kin,
Their eyes scanning the sky, hoping to find therein
The inspiration to rekindle absent dreams.

The cricket, in the recess of his sandy lair,
Sees them pass by and greets them with a cheerful air,
While Cybele, who loves them, makes the landscape green,

And cleaves the desert rock to make a flowing tide
For those tired travellers, to whom is opened wide
The gateway to a future life as yet unseen.

XVI. — MAN AND THE SEA

Free man, you will forever venerate the sea!
It is your looking glass; you contemplate your soul
In its depths, as its never-ending billows roll,
And the tide of your thoughts flows no less bitterly.

For solace you are wont on your image to gaze.
You embrace it with eyes and arms, and your sad heart
Is oftentimes assuaged of its own aching smart
By the plaintive lament of the unfurling waves.

The two of you are both tenebrous and discreet:
Man, you have yet your deepest secrets to reveal.
O Sea, nobody knows the riches you conceal,
So jealous are you of the secrets you both keep!

Yet since the dawn of time you have fought bitterly,
Relentlessly and without pity or regret,
So strong is your desire for carnage and for death,
O unrelenting foes, brothers in enmity!

XVII. – DON JUAN IN HELL

When Don Juan had descended to the subterranean sea,
And paid the ferryman the halfpenny he owed,
A swarthy mendicant, proud as Antisthenes,
Seizing both oars, made vengeful gestures as he rowed.

And through unfastened robes displaying hanging breasts,
Women twisted and writhed beneath a stygian sky,
And like a lowing herd of sacrificial beasts,
Followed behind him with a long and plaintive cry.

A laughing Sganarelle was asking for his wage,
While Don Luis, with all the dead assembled there,
Pointed a trembling finger, with barely hidden rage,
At the audacious son who had mocked his white hair.

Elvira, chaste and gaunt, shuddered in sorrow, while,
Beside the faithless spouse who'd once her lover been,
She seemed to ask of him, for one last time, a smile
Wherein to find the warmth that her eyes once had seen.

Erect, in armour clad, a man, hewn out of stone,
Stood at the helm and cut a passage through the haze.
But the calm hero, leaning on his sword, alone,
His eyes fixed on the wake, did not avert his gaze.

XVIII. — PUNISHMENT OF PRIDE

In those exalted times in which Theology
Flourished with ardent zeal and fervent energy,
A great and learned doctor, so the tale imparts,
— Having forced learned doctrines on indifferent hearts,
And stirred within them thoughts tenebrous and profound,
And having traversed strange and unfamiliar ground
In search of heavenly glories yet to him unknown,
To which only pure Spirits ever could have flown, —
Having aspired too high, in panic and distress
Cried out, with arrogant, satanic bitterness:
"Jesus, my little Jesus, I brought you great renown!
But, had I wished, I could have brought you crashing down,
Through chinks in your defence your glory brought to shame,
And you'd be just an embryo without a name!"

And even as he spoke his reason took its leave.
The brightness of his sun was veiled in a naïve,
Chaotic cloud of doubt; and his intelligence,
Erstwhile a living temple, full of opulence,
Beneath whose dome had shone such majesty and pride,
Became a place where only darkness could reside,
A silent sepulchre to which there was no key.
From then on, like a stray dog, wandering aimlessly
Across the countryside, traversing vale and hill,
Unable to tell summer's heat from winter's chill,
Dishevelled and unwashed, his aspect was so grim
That laughing children would delight in mocking him.

XIX. — BEAUTY

I'm beautiful, O mortals, like a dream in stone!
My breast, where men have suffered, each one in his turn,
Inspires within the poet love that's taciturn,
Eternal as the substance from which it is hewn.

Like a mysterious sphinx I rule the azure sky;
A heart of snow with swanlike whiteness I combine;
I shun all movement that mars purity of line,
And never do I laugh and never do I cry.

Poets, entranced by my demeanour, will revere
A bearing borrowed from the finest monuments,
And spend their days engrossed in study most austere,

For I possess, to charm those docile supplicants,
Pure mirrors that make all things fairer to their sight:
My eyes, wide eyes that radiate eternal light!

XX. — THE IDEAL

It never will be those false beauties of vignettes,
Those products of a worthless era's poor design,
Those feet in ankle-boots, fingers in castanets,
That will know how to satisfy a heart like mine.

I leave to Gavarni, the poet of chlorosis,
His prattling herd of so-called beauties, sick and weak,
For I shall never find among those pale roses
A flower that reveals the ideal red I seek.

What's needed for this heart, profound as endless time,
Is you, Lady Macbeth, a soul potent in crime,
A dream of Aeschylus born in storm-winds from the south;

Or you, great Night, daughter of Michelangelo,
Who twist so peacefully into a curious show
Your charms that were engendered in the Titan's mouth!

XXI. — THE GIANTESS

In times when Nature's zeal was given to excess,
And every day brought forth infants of monstrous mien,
I should like to have lived with a young giantess,
Like a voluptuous cat at the feet of a queen.

I would have loved to watch her body grow in size
And flourish with her spirit in fantastic games,
And in the humid mists that hovered in her eyes
Divine if in her heart there smouldered darker flames.

About her wondrous form to wander as I please,
To clamber on the slopes of her enormous knees,
And when, wearied by summer's heat, she takes her rest,

Stretched out across the land in slumber calm and still,
To sleep without a care in the shade of her breast,
Like a small hamlet nestling underneath a hill.

XXII. — THE PROMISES OF A FACE

I love, O beauty pale, your eyes, as they look down,
And from which darkness seems to flow.
Your eyes inspire in me, though they are darkest brown,
Thoughts where contentment seems to glow.

Your eyes, which are in harmony with your black hair,
Those tresses supple and profuse,
Your eyes, so languidly, say to me: "If you dare,
Admirer of the plastic muse,

To follow every hope that in you we have stirred,
And all that might enchant your eyes,
You now may see the truth and honour of our word
Between the navel and the thighs.

You will find at the tip of each voluptuous breast,
A large medallion of bronze,
And under a smooth abdomen, soft as velour
And dark as the skin of a bonze,

A fleece, capacious, rich, that truly is the twin,
The equal in sublime delight,
Of this abundant hair, whose thickness is akin
To yours, O Night, black, starless Night!"

XXIII. — THE JEWELS

My dearest love was naked, and, knowing my heart,
Had kept as sole attire her most sonorous gems,
Whose opulent display resembled the proud art
Of Moorish concubines bedecked with diadems.

When, shaken, it emits a lively mocking sound,
This radiant world of metal and resplendent stone
Fills me with ecstasy, for I have always found
Joy in the subtle interplay of light and tone.

And there she lay in languorous cupidity,
Smiling as she looked down upon her willing slave,
Upon my love, as deep as the eternal sea,
That flowed toward her being, as to the cliffs the wave.

Like a tame tiger, gazing at me fixedly,
She dreamily adopted miscellaneous poses,
Combining artlessness with impropriety,
Which lent a novel charm to her metamorphoses.

And her arms and her legs, and her loins and her thighs,
Undulating, swanlike, with softly silken sheen,
Serenely passed before my penetrating eyes.
And her belly and breasts, those sweet grapes of my vine,

Advanced, like wanton Angels in their sweet allure,
Disturbing the repose in which my soul had been,
And shattering the rock of crystal clear and pure
On which she had reposed, solitary and serene.

I thought I saw, united in a new design,
Antiope's ample hips with the bust of a boy,
The slimness of her waist lending her pelvic shrine
More prominence; and its dark colouring, what joy!

— As the bedchamber's lamplight was resigned to die,
Only the glowing hearth lit up the space therein,
And every time it uttered a flamboyant sigh,
It emblazoned with blood her amber-coloured skin!

XXIV. — THE MASK
Allegorical statue in the Renaissance style

To Ernest Christophe, sculptor

Let's contemplate this gem of Florentine design.
In the curves of this form, so lithe and powerful,
Abound both Elegance and Strength, sisters divine.
This woman, art in stone, creative miracle,
Divinely slender and adorably robust,
Would grace a pontiff's couch, or merit pride of place
Upon a sumptuous bed, to charm a prince's lust.

— And see the subtle smile that lights her lovely face,
Where proud Conceit displays its noble ecstasy;
That sly, lingering look, mocking and languorous;
That charming countenance, gauze-framed so daintily,
Whose every feature says, proud and victorious:
"Indulgence beckons me, and Love ennobles me!"
To such a being, favoured with such stateliness,
See what exciting charm is lent by sympathy!
Let us approach, and marvel in her loveliness.

O blasphemy of art! Fatal epiphany!
This body so divine, that promised such delight,
Is topped by a bicephalous monstrosity!

— But no! It's just a mask, a fantasy of sight,
That face illumined by an exquisite grimace,
For look: here we can see, convulsed atrociously,
The bona fide head, with the authentic face
Reversed, concealed behind the face of perfidy.
O beauty so defiled! your flowing tears awake
Such turmoil in my heart; bewildered by these lies,
My soul must drink its fill, its ardent thirst to slake,
From that great flood of Sorrow streaming from your eyes!

— But wherefore does she weep? She who, so wondrous fair,
Could prostrate at her feet the conquered human race,
What enigmatic torment brings her such despair?

— She weeps, you fool, because life has gone on apace!
And she still lives today! But what gives her most pain,
What makes her body tremble to its very core
Is that, alas, tomorrow she must live again!
Tomorrow and tomorrow! Like us — for evermore!

XXV. — HYMN TO BEAUTY

Did you descend from heaven, or rise from the abyss,
O Beauty? Your demeanour, infernal and divine,
Mingles confusedly iniquity and bliss,
Wherefore you surely may be likened unto wine.

Your eyes are home to both the sunset and aurora.
You scatter wide your perfumes like a stormy night.
Your kisses are a philtre and your mouth an amphora,
Which rouse a child yet cause a hero to take flight.

Are you from the black depths or from the stars of light?
Charmed Destiny pursues you like a faithful hound.
You scatter as you please both sorrow and delight,
Commanding everything and yet by nothing bound.

You trample on the dead, and show disdain for them.
Among your baubles Dread reserves a special place,
And Murder, of your charms perhaps the finest gem,
On your proud belly dances with erotic grace.

The dazzled moth flies blindly to the candle's light,
Crackles and burns and says: Bless this torch of my doom!
The panting lover, lying with his bride at night,
Is like a dying man caressing his own tomb.

What matter that you come from heaven or from hell,
O Beauty! dreadful, huge, naïve monstrosity!
If your eyes or your smile my spirit can propel
Into an Infinite as yet unknown to me?

From Satan or from God, who cares? Angel or Sprite,
What does it matter, if you make, — silken-eyed fay,
Unique and glorious queen, rhythm, aroma, light! —
The world less hideous and the moments less grey?

XXVI. — EXOTIC FRAGRANCE

When I, with shuttered eyes, on a warm autumn night,
Inhale the stunning fragrance of your fond embrace,
I see the blissful shores of an exotic place,
Illumined by an ardent sun's unchanging light.

An isle of indolence where nature's panoply
Reveals fantastic trees, with luscious fruits weighed down;
Men that are vigorous, with bodies lithe and brown;
Women whose eyes astound with their sincerity.

Guided by your aromas to such charming climes,
I see a port with sails and masts in its confines,
Still weary from their labours in the ocean's swell,

While the sweet fragrance of the verdant tamarind,
That fills my nostrils with its aromatic smell,
Drifts with the boatman's song upon a zephyr wind.

XXVII. — THE HEAD OF HAIR

O tresses that enfold your shoulders with such grace!
O curls! O fragrance wafting nonchalantly there!
What rapture! And to fill the boudoir's sombre space
With memories that sleep in this luxuriant place,
I want to shake it like a kerchief in the air!

Asia, where languor dwells, Africa's scorching heat,
Those distant worlds, whose absent wonders are so rare,
Live in the depths of this ambrosial retreat!
While other spirits float on sounds of music sweet,
Mine, O my love! bathes in the perfume of your hair.

I'll go where trees and men live in serenity,
Beneath an ardent sun taking their languid ease.
Thick tresses, be the swell that lifts and carries me!
You hold, ebony sea, a dazzling reverie,
Of masts and sails afloat upon a zephyr breeze:

A busy haven where my spirit can inhale
A flood of sound and colour, fragrance, purity,
Where vessels glide on seas of amber in full sail,
Unfolding wide their arms to greet the majesty
Of a pure sky where warmth resides eternally.

And I shall plunge my head in eager drunkenness
Into this black sea where the other is enclosed,
And my keen spirit, that the gentle waves caress,
Will know where you reside, O fecund idleness,
Eternal lullaby of sweet-scented repose!

Blue tresses, darkly flowing like a banner, where
I revel in the azure blue of skies afar;
Upon the downy fringes of your tangled hair
I ardently imbibe the mingled perfumes there,
The oil of coconut, the heady musk and tar.

Always! forever! in your flowing locks entwined,
My hand will sow pearls, rubies, sapphires crystalline,
So that to my desire you never will be blind!
Are you not the oasis where I dream, the vine
From which I take long draughts of your nostalgic wine?

XXVIII.

I love you as I love the starlit firmament,
O distant, silent one, O vase of discontent,
And I love you the more because you flee from me,
Because it seems, adornment of my nights, that you
Accumulate the leagues, O cruel irony,
That separate my arms from the eternal blue.

And I mount an assault, advancing to attack,
Like a platoon of maggots on a corpse's back,
And I hold dear, O beast cruel and implacable!
Even that chill which renders you more beautiful!

XXIX.

You'd take the entire universe into your shrine,
Lewd woman! Boredom makes your spirit so malign.
To exercise your teeth in this singular play,
You need a new heart in your manger every day.
Your eyes, afire like a shop window filled with light,
Or like a blazing yew tree on a festive night,
Abuse their borrowed power with impunity,
Oblivious to the laws that govern their beauty.

O blind and deaf machine, with cruelty aflood!
Vigorous instrument, imbiber of man's blood,
How can you have no shame, and why do they conceal,
Those mirrors where you gaze, your withering appeal?
Has this great evil, you who think you are so wise,
Not caused you once to flinch before its very size,
When nature, so immense in its arcane design,
Makes use of you, O queen of all that is malign,
— Of you, vile animal, — to mould a prodigy?

Contemptible grandeur! Sublime ignominy!

XXX. — SED NON SATIATA

Bizarre goddess, whose hair is black as darkest night,
With mingled fragrances of musk and havana,
The work of some obi, Faust of the savannah,
Ebony sorceress, child of the black midnight,

I love, more than constantia, opium, côte-de-nuits,
The liquor of your lips where love's conceits parade.
When my desires toward you move in cavalcade,
Your eyes become the spring that quenches my ennui.

From those dark eyes, those windows of your soul's desire,
O demon without grace, pour me less ardent fire!
I'm not the River Styx, nine times to circle you,

Alas! and I cannot, Megaera libertine,
To weaken your defence and triumph over you,
In your infernal bed become a Proserpine!

XXXI.

To see her undulating, opalescent dress,
You'd think, as she walks by, that she's about to dance,
Like snakes that street performers show off to impress,
Adroitly waving sticks to put them in a trance.

Like endless azure skies above bleak desert sand,
Both unaware of human suffering and despair,
Like wave on endless wave breaking far from the land,
She goes about her life, it seems, without a care.

Her shining eyes are made of crystals pure and bright,
And in that strange, symbolic temperament that links
The inviolate angel and the fabled sphinx,

Where all is gold, and steel, and diamonds, and light,
There shines, like a vain star, for all eternity,
The sterile woman's regal, frigid majesty.

XXXII. — THE DANCING SERPENT

My languid love, how I admire
Your form so lithe and slim,
And, like a mesh of golden wire,
The shimmer of your skin!

Upon your deep, abundant hair,
With its pungent scent,
Fragrant flowing ocean where
Azure waves augment,

Like a vessel that awakes
To the morning breeze,
My quixotic spirit takes
Off on distant seas.

Your eyes, which neither gentleness
Nor bitterness reveal,
Are like two precious gems that blend
Gold with icy steel.

The carefree rhythm in your gait
Would seem to correspond
To that of a dancing snake
Enchanted by a wand.

Beneath the weight of idleness,
Your head, my sweet infant,
Moves freely, with the suppleness
Of a young elephant.

Your body leans and stretches forth
Like a ship on the lee,
Rolling from side to side to dip
Its yardarm in the sea.

Like waters swollen by the thaw
Of an icy reef,
When your saliva rises up
Against your opal teeth,

I taste a fine Bohemian wine,
Powerful and tart,
A liquid paradise divine
That sows stars in my heart!

XXXIII. — A CARRION

Remember, O my soul, the object that we saw
One lovely tranquil summer's day:
Upon a bed of stones a corpse, rotting and raw,
Before us on the footpath lay.

Legs in the air, resembling a lubricious whore,
With sweating poisons overrun,
Nonchalantly displaying, with a stench of gore,
Its reeking belly to the sun.

The sun shone fiercely down on this putridity
As if to cook it thoroughly,
And so give back to Nature the entirety
Of what she'd fashioned lovingly.

The sky beheld the place where this fine carrion lay
As if it were a flower in bloom.
So noisome was the stench of that obscene decay
You felt you were about to swoon.

The flies buzzed busily around that rotting belly,
From which there came black regiments
Of larvae that flowed forth like a thick viscous jelly
Among those living excrements.

Like an unfurling wave the whole thing rose and fell,
Or burst out in a bubbling spray.
You might say that the corpse appeared to breathe and swell,
Regenerating where it lay.

And this world gave forth music, full of mystery,
Like flowing water and the wind,
Or grain the winnower, with rhythmic artistry,
Shakes and rotates in his bin.

The outlines disappeared, remaining but a dream,
A hazy sketch in muted tones
On a forgotten canvas, that the artist might seem
To paint from memory alone.

And from behind a rock an agitated bitch
Was watching us resentfully,
Waiting to take back from the corpse the morsel which
She had let fall so carelessly.

— And yet you will one day be like this carrion too,
This horrible contamination,
O bright star of my eyes, sun of my nature, you,
My angel and my exaltation!

Yes! that is how you'll be, O queen of every grace,
After your last rites have been said,
When you are laid to rest in a calm, verdant place,
To rot with the bones of the dead.

And then say to the worms and vermin, beauty mine!
Whose kisses gorge on your allures,
That I have kept the form and the essence divine
Of all my decomposed amours!

XXXIV. – A SAD MADRIGAL

I

What do I care if you are wise?
Be beautiful! Be sad! It's plain
That tears add magic to your eyes,
As rivers grace the countryside
And flow'rs are freshened by the rain.

I love to see your joy depart
When your demeanor is downcast;
When horror suffocates your heart ;
When present time is torn apart
By dreadful shadows of the past.

I love you when, in your distress,
Your tears, warm as your blood, are shed;
When, notwithstanding my caress,
The plaintive sounds of your distress
Are like rales from a hospice bed.

And I inhale, divine delight!
Exquisite hymn, profound and wise!
The sobs that from your breast arise,
And sense your heart is bathed in light
From pearls cascading from your eyes.

II

I know your heart is still possessed
By former loves now cast aside,
That the old ardour does not rest
And that you harbour in your breast
The remnants of damnations's pride.

But, dearest, so long as your dreams
Have not reflected Hell's appeal,
If your relentless nightmare seems
To be obsessed with ghastly schemes
Of poison, gunpowder and steel;

If, dreading every caller's knock,
Regarding all things as unjust,
Recoiling from the chiming clock,
You've not been held within the lock
Of irresistible Disgust,

You cannot, O my queen and slave,
Whose love can only terror bring,
In darkness awful as the grave
Say to me, with a heart that's brave:
"I am your equal, O my King!"

XXXV. — DE PROFUNDIS CLAMAVI

My one and only love, I beg pity of Thee,
From the deep, dark abyss in which my heart now lies,
A universe of gloom beset by leaden skies,
Where every night is filled with dread and blasphemy.

A cold sun hovers overhead for half the year;
The other half is shrouded in obscurity,
O'er land more barren than the pole's immensity:
 — No sign of beast nor verdure, stream nor woodland here!

There is no horror in the world that could outrun
The numbing cruelty of this hibernal sun
And this vast night, like Chaos in the myths of old.

I'm envious of the lot of those beasts of the fold
That sleep without a care, to their destiny blind,
So slowly does the endless skein of time unwind!

XXXVI. — THE VAMPIRE

You who, like the thrust of a knife
Entered into my plaintive heart;
You who came into my sad life
Your mad adornments to impart,

And of my subjugated soul
To make your bed and your domain,
Vile creature whom I must extol,
Tied like a convict to his chain,

Or like a gambler to the dice,
Or like a drunkard to his flask,
Or like a carrion to its lice
— May you be cursed, that's all I ask!

I have entreated the swift sword
To give me back my liberty.
The poisoned chalice I've implored
To banish my timidity.

Alas! The poison and the blade
Showed me disdain and said to me:
"You are not worthy to be freed
From your accursed slavery,

Imbecile! — If from her empire
Your soul we were to liberate,
Your kisses would resuscitate
The cadaver of your vampire!"

XXXVII. — THE LETHE

Unyielding soul, come to my heart again,
Beloved tigress with your languid air,
I want to plunge my trembling fingers there
In the deep ocean of your heavy mane.

And in your skirts, filled with your scent, to hide
My aching head as in a secret bower,
And breathe once more, as from a withered flower,
The gentle fragrance of a love that died.

I want to sleep, rather than live, alas!
In slumber that is bittersweet as death,
I'll spread without remorse my soft caress
Upon your body smooth as polished brass.

To drown my muted sobs there's no abyss
That equals the deep haven of your breast.
Your lips speak of oblivion's sweet rest,
And silent Lethe courses in your kiss.

To my destiny, henceforth my delight,
My staunch obedience is preordained.
A docile martyr who's unjustly blamed,
Whose fervour serves to amplify his plight,

I'll suck, to drown my rancour's aching smart,
Nepenthe and the hemlock's bitter zest
From the sweet promontories of this breast,
That never gave asylum to a heart.

XXXVIII.

One night as I lay with a dreadful Jewish whore,
Like a cadaver that a fellow corpse has sought,
I called to mind, beside that body I had bought,
The beauty my desire was destined to ignore.

I saw in my mind's eye her native majesty,
Her candid gaze, so full of energy and grace,
Her hair, a perfumed hood that frames her lovely face,
Of which my heart retains the ardent memory.

For fain would I have kissed a body I revere,
And from your fragrant feet to your obsidian tresses,
Unleashed the treasury of my profound caresses,

If, one night, you could just have shed one artless tear,
O queen whose cruelty your beauty so belies,
To dull the splendour of your cold uncaring eyes.

XXXIX. — POSTHUMOUS REMORSE

My beauty dark, when you lie in eternal sleep,
Deep in a sepulchre of black marble and stone,
And when all that you have for bedchamber and home
Is but a leaking tomb within a hollow deep;

When the stone, pressing down upon your anxious breast
And your limbs, rendered supple by sweet nonchalance,
Prevents your heart from beating and, stifling your will,
Stops your feet from pursuing their intrepid quest,

The tomb, companion of my never-ending dream
(For tombs will always understand the poet's pain),
Throughout those endless nights that sleep cannot redeem,

Will ask: "What does it profit you, flawed courtesan,
Not to have known what causes dead men's tears to course?"
— And worms will gnaw you as a token of remorse.

XL. — THE CAT

Come, my fine cat, onto my loving heart.
Take care your talons to conceal,
And let your mystic eyes to me impart
Their gaze of agate and of steel.

When my keen fingertips caress at leisure
Your neck's smooth elasticity,
And when my hand palpates with drunken pleasure
Your body's electricity,

I call to mind the mistress of my heart.
Her gaze, like yours, congenial beast,
Is cold, profound and piercing as a dart,

And, from her tresses to her feet
A dangerous perfume, a subtle air,
Hovers about her body there.

XLI. — DUELLUM

Two warriors rushed towards each other, and their arms
Flashed brightly in the air and spattered it with blood.
This sport, this clattering of steel, are the alarms
Of youth that's fallen prey to the first pangs of love.

The weapons are now broken, like our youth, sweet maid!
But teeth and fingernails, with likewise cruel intent,
Will soon avenge the sword and the perfidious blade.
O wrath of ageing hearts by love's afflictions rent!

Into the gorge where lynx and panther strut their power
Our heroes have careered, locked in a fierce embrace,
And on the arid thorns their shredded skin will flower.

— Into this gulf, this hell, our common dwelling-place,
Let's go, inhuman amazon, without remorse,
There to perpetuate our hatred's ardent force!

XLII. — THE BALCONY

Mother of memories, mistress of mistresses,
O you my every bliss, O you my every duty,
You will recall the joy of our fervent caresses,
The comfort of the hearth, the evening's tranquil beauty,
Mother of memories, mistress of mistresses!

The evenings by the fire, lit by the burning coal,
And on the balcony, veiled in a rosy hue,
The softness of your breast, the sweetness of your soul!
We said so many things that are forever true,
The evenings by the fire, lit by the burning coal!

How beautiful the sunlight on a summer's night!
How deep the vault of heaven! How strong the beating heart!
Holding you close to me, O queen of my delight,
It seemed your very blood did its sweet scent impart.
How beautiful the sunlight on a summer's night!

The wall of darkness thickened, shutting out the light,
And in the gloom my eyes sought your eyes longingly,
And I imbibed your breath, O poisonous delight!
And in my loving hands your feet slept peacefully.
The wall of darkness thickened, shutting out the light.

The recollection of sweet moments is an art
That lets me live again those hours of happiness.
Why should I seek elsewhere than in your loving heart,
And in your gracious form, the joys of languidness?
The recollection of sweet moments is an art!

Those vows, those fragrant scents, those kisses without end,
Can they be born again from gulfs we cannot sound,
Just as the endless seas back to the heavens send
Rejuvenated suns that from their depths rebound?
 — O vows! O fragrant scents! O kisses without end!

XLIII. — THE POSSESSED

The sun has donned a veil of mourning. Just as he
Has done, Moon of my life! be clothed in shadow too.
Sleep or smoke as you wish; be silent as you do,
And sink into the depths of infinite Ennui.

I love you thus! However, if you wish today,
Like an eclipsed star that emerges from the dark,
To flaunt yourself where Folly goes to leave its mark,
That's fine! Knife, leave your scabbard! Go your charming way!

Let your eyes in the chandelier's light come ablaze!
Ignite desire within the eyes of old roués!
Despondent or perverse: what you are, I adore.

Be what you will, black night, or new dawn's scarlet hue;
There's not a single fibre in my trembling core
That does not cry *Beelzebub, I worship you!*

XLIV. — A PHANTOM

I. The Shadows

In the deep vaults of fathomless distress
To which Fate has already banished me;
Where not a ray of sunlight do I see;
Where, lonely with the Night, morose hostess,

I'm like an artist that God mockingly
Condemns to paint on shadows, without light;
Where, like a cook with morbid appetite,
I boil and eat my own heart secretly.

At times a spectral form in that dark place
Appears, and spreads itself before my eyes.
In its exquisite oriental grace,

When it has grown to reach its fullest size,
I recognise this visitor most fair:
It's Her! dark-hued yet radiant, standing there.

II. The Perfume

Reader, have you perchance sometimes at dusk
With gentle delectation caught a wave
Of heady incense that pervades a nave,
Or from a sachet smelt the timeless musk?

Profound, intoxicating sorcery,
The past transported to the present time!
As when the lover from a form sublime
Plucks the exquisite flower of memory.

From the thick tresses of her supple hair,
Living sachet, the boudoir's incense urn,
Arose a fragrance, wild as forest fern,

And, impregnated with her youth so fair,
Her clothes, that were of muslin or velour,
Exhaled an odour redolent of fur.

III. The Frame

Just as a frame around a work of art,
Even one painted by a famous hand,
Detaches it from the surrounding land,
A strange, magical beauty to impart,

So gemstones, metals, gold accoutrements
Ably accompanied her artistry.
Nothing could obfuscate her purity,
And all things served her as embellishments.

You might have sometimes even said she thought
That she was loved by all things, as she sought
To drown her nakedness indulgently

In kisses of fine linen, silk and crepe,
And with each movement, swift or leisurely,
Displayed the childlike grace of a young ape.

IV. The Portrait

Disease and Death reduce to ash and cinder
Our passion that once burned with ardent fire.
Of those wide eyes so fervent and so tender,
That mouth where my heart drowned in deep desire,

Of those clandestine kisses that we stole,
Those transports more intense than lambent rays,
What now remains? It's awful, O my soul!
Just a three-coloured sketch, a pallid haze,

Which, like me, dies and slowly fades away,
And which harsh Time, malignant patriarch,
Abrades with his rough pinion every day...

Killer of Life and Art, assassin dark,
You'll never banish from my memory
The one who was my joy and majesty!

XLV.

I offer you these verses so that if my renown
Should happily approach the shores of distant days,
And cause to dream new human spirits with my lays,
Like a ship on whose sails the northern wind bears down,

Your memory, like hazy myths from bygone times,
Will lull the reader with a dulcimer-like sound,
And by a mystic link, fraternal and profound,
Remain as if suspended from my haughty rhymes.

Accursèd one to whom nothing but me replies,
From the profound abyss to the most distant skies!
— O you who, like a shadow's ephemeral trace,

Tread lightly underfoot, as you serenely pass,
The stupid mortals who know nothing of your grace,
Statue with eyes of jet, angel with brow of brass!

XLVI. — SEMPER EADEM

You asked: "How did this strange despondency begin,
Which rises like a wave on some dark distant reef?"
— When the grapes of our heart have all been gathered in,
We know that life henceforth will bring us only grief.

The pain is very simple, there's no mystery,
And, like your joy, it's very plain for all to see.
Abandon then your search, O curious beauty!
And, though your voice be gentle, let it silent be!

Be silent, foolish soul with rapture ever rife!
Infantile smiling face! Far more even than Life,
The subtle bonds of Death often around us twine.

Now let my heart the heady wine of *falsehood* drink,
Into your lovely eyes as in a daydream sink,
And in the shadow of your lashes long recline!

XLVII. — ALL OF HER

The Devil came to call on me
This morning in my attic room,
And, seeking to befuddle me,
Said: "Tell me, if I may presume,

Among the wonders that compose
The beauty of her form so fair,
Among the objects black or rose
That lend her such a charming air,

Which is the sweetest?" — O my Soul!
You did reply to the Abhorred:
"In truth, she is a perfect whole:
Each virtue brings its own reward.

Her every feature gives delight —
What charms me most? I do not know.
She is the solace of the Night,
The radiance of Aurora's glow.

A most exquisite harmony
Pervades the union of her arts,
And no impotent scrutiny
Can separate the diverse parts.

O mystic metamorphosis
Of every sense uniquely blent!
Her breath is music's synthesis,
And her voice gives forth fragrant scent!"

XLVIII. — HYMN

To her most dear, to her most fair
Who fills my heart with clarity,
To an angel beyond compare,
Greetings in immortality!

She flows into my consciousness
Like a salt breeze's soft caress,
And into my unsated soul
She pours a taste of timelessness.

Ever fresh sachet which perfumes
A treasured place with sweet delight,
Forgotten incense bowl which fumes
In secrecy throughout the night,

How, love that's incorruptible,
Can I describe you truthfully?
A grain of musk, invisible,
Deep in my soul's eternity!

To her most dear, to her most fair,
My joy and my felicity,
To an angel beyond compare,
Greetings in immortality!

XLIX.

What will you say tonight, poor solitary soul,
What will you say, my heart, once so enmeshed in gloom,
To her who is so dear, so good, so beautiful,
Whose countenance divine has made your spirit bloom?

— We'll harness all our pride to sing her highest praise.
Nothing can match the grace of her authority.
Her mystic flesh is perfumed by angelic rays,
And her eyes clothe us in a robe of clarity.

Be it at dead of night and in deep solitude,
Or in the city streets among the multitude,
Her phantom, like a torch, is on the ether blown.

Sometimes it speaks: "I'm beautiful, and I decree
That for the love of me you love Beauty alone.
Madonna, guardian Angel, Muse — I am all three."

L. — THE LIVING TORCH

Before me they advance, those eyes ablaze with light,
Eyes that a learned Angel doubtless magnetized,
Celestial brothers, my own brothers, burning bright,
Their diamantine flame reflecting in my eyes.

Preserving me from snares and from all error grave,
Along the path of Beauty they show me the way.
They are my servitors and I their humble slave,
A living torch that my whole being must obey.

Beguiling Eyes, you have the mystic clarity
Of candles glowing in the light of day; the sun
Burns bright but does not quell their luminosity.

While *they* laud Death, *you* sing of a new day begun:
My soul's awakening is the anthem you proclaim,
Bright stars of which no sun could ever dull the flame!

LI. — TO HER WHO IS TOO GAY

Your head, your bearing, and your grace
Are like a charming landscape where,
Like zephyr breezes in the air,
Sweet laughter plays upon your face.

Sad souls you pass along the way
Are dazzled by the radiant health
That shines in such abundant wealth
From your sublime décolleté.

Resplendent colours that enhance
The beauty of your fine array
Inspire upon the poet's eye
The image of a floral dance.

These mad creations symbolise
The multi-coloured spirit of
A woman whom I madly love,
And also hate, in equal wise!

Oft, in a garden seeking rest,
I dragged my sluggish atony,
And felt the bitter irony
Of sunlight tearing at my breast.

And springtime's green magnificence
Cast such despair upon my heart,
That on a flower I did impart
Revenge for Nature's insolence.

Therefore, one night, clandestinely,
When sounds the hour of volupty,
Into your carnal treasury
I'll creep, a coward, silently,

There to chastise your blissful flesh,
To bruise your now forgiven breast,
And carve on your astonished side
An open wound both deep and wide,

And, heady sweetness that enthrals!
Into those fresh lips' gaping walls,
Where new joys and delights appear,
To spurt my venom, sister dear!

LII. — REVERSIBILITY

Angel of gaiety, what know you of distress,
Of shame, remorse, vexation, tears of misery,
And of those dreadful nights the vague anxiety
That, like a crumpled leaf, the troubled heart compress?
Angel of gaiety, what know you of distress?

Angel of charity, what do you know of hate,
Fists clenched in darkness, eyes that weep the tears of gall,
When Vengeance beats the drum that sounds the dreadful call,
And makes himself the prince and captain of our fate?
Angel of charity, what do you know of hate?

Angel of health, what do you know of Fever's pain,
Fever that trails along the hospice's pale walls,
Like an outcast who drags his limbs, and limps and crawls,
Moving his lips while seeking rays of light in vain?
Angel of health, what do you know of Fever's pain?

Angel of beauty, do you know senility,
The fear of growing old, the hideous emotion
When we discern the secret horror of devotion
In eyes where for so long our eyes drank eagerly!
Angel of beauty, do you know senility?

Angel of rapture, joy and luminosity,
The dying David surely would have asked to share
The mystic emanations of your form so fair;
But all I ask, angel, is that you pray for me,
Angel of rapture, joy and luminosity!

LIII. — CONFESSION

Once, just once, sweet and gentle woman, did you place
Your silken arm upon my own
(From my soul's most profound and most secretive space
That memory has never flown);

'Twas late; and like a gleaming new medallion
The full moon in the heavens glowed,
And, over sleeping Paris holding dominion,
Solemn night like a river flowed.

Among the houses and beneath the porticos,
The prowling cats passed furtively,
With ears pricked up, or else, like the shadows of those
Most dear, walked with us silently.

Suddenly, in the midst of this intimacy
That blossomed in the pale moonlight,
From you, sonorous instrument whose gaiety
Rang out so clearly in the night,

From you, clear, joyous, like a fanfare from afar
Resounding in the sparkling morn,
A note that was most plaintive, a note most bizarre,
Escaped, faltering and forlorn,

As if from some deformed, pathetic, sickly child,
Whose kin would be so mortified
She would be hidden from a world where she's reviled,
And in a cellar cast aside.

Poor angel, thus it sang, your strangely piercing note:
"In this world lives no certainty
And, though it would an air of sympathy promote,
Man's selfishness is plain to see.

What a harsh task it is to be a woman fair,
And with what banal nonchalance
The dancing girl, with a cold and impartial air,
Must smile as if in penitence.

To build on human hearts is a most foolish thing:
All things must cede, love and beauty,
Until Oblivion consigns them to his bin
And sends them to Eternity!"

I often have recalled the moon's magnificence
That such enchantment did impart,
And that disturbing, whispered, secret utterance
From the confessional of the heart.

LIV. — SPIRITUAL DAWN

When on a debauchee Aurora's pale dawn breaks
And meets with the Ideal that's wont his heart to gnaw,
By operation of a vengeful secret law
Within the drowsy brute a dormant angel wakes.

The unreachable blue of the Ethereal Skies,
For him who suffers still, though he would dream of bliss,
Opens and sinks with the allure of the abyss.
Therefore, beloved Goddess, Being pure and wise,

Above the murky dross of revelry and shame,
The thought of you, beguiling in its clarity,
Before my startled eyes pulsates incessantly.

The sun has rendered black the dying candle's flame.
Thus, ever conquering, your phantom is at one,
Resplendent Entity, with the immortal sun!

LV. — EVENING HARMONY

The time of year has come when on warm summer days
Each flower spreads its scent like a censer of gold.
The sounds and fragrances in harmony enfold
The melancholic languor of the evening haze!

Each flower spreads its scent like a censer of gold.
Like an afflicted heart the trembling fiddle plays.
O melancholic languor of the evening haze!
The firmament is like a great altar of gold.

Like an afflicted heart the trembling fiddle plays,
A tender heart that hates the black void to behold!
The firmament is like a great altar of gold.
The sun drowns in the blood of its vermilion rays.

A tender heart, which hates the black void to behold,
Remembers every vestige of past happy days!
The sun drowns in the blood of its vermilion rays...
Your memory shines in me like a monstrance of gold!

LVI. — THE FLASK

There are strong perfumes which can penetrate all mass.
It seems all things to them are porous, even glass.
On opening a coffer brought home from the East
Whose lock creaks as in protest when it is released,

Or in a long-abandoned house a cabinet,
Dusty and black, with the dank smell of time beset,
We sometimes find an ancient bottle which might host
The living, breathing soul of a returning ghost.

Like dormant chrysalids a thousand thoughts lie there,
Pulsating silently in their tenebrous lair,
And then, to take their flight, their azure wings unfold,
Wings that are glazed with rose and embroidered with gold.

Intoxicating memories escape, flutter and rise
In the nebulous air; we blink, and close our eyes;
Vertigo grips the soul and sends it hurtling down
Into a dark abyss where human scents abound.

And it is in that dark abyss that we might meet,
Like reeking Lazarus tearing his winding-sheet,
The ghostly cadaver of a rancid old flame
That rises from its slumber on hearing its name.

Therefore, when long forgotten by men, I am thrown
Into the corner of some cupboard, lost, alone,
A desolate old flask, powdery, caked in dirt,
Slimy, abject, opaque, decrepit, cracked, inert,

I'll be your coffin, O delightful pestilence!
The witness of your force and of your virulence,
Dear poison made by angels, whose liquescent fire
Gnaws at my heart, O life and death of my desire!

LVII. — THE POISON

Wine knows how to embellish the most sordid room
With a luxurious disguise,
Making the most fantastic colonnades arise
In the gold of its crimson bloom,
Like the sun's dying rays suffusing misty skies.

Opium magnifies that which is limitless,
Extends beyond infinity,
Amplifies time, intensifies cupidity,
And with thrills dark and joyless
Pervades the soul beyond its full capacity.

Yet neither can compete with the poison that flows
From your eyes, your green eyes so fair,
Lakes where my soul recoils from its reflection there...
My dreams have no repose
And to those bitter gulfs in multitudes repair.

There's nothing that can match the terrible prowess
Of your saliva and your breath,
Which cast into oblivion my soul without redress,
Depriving it of consciousness,
And pushing it, defenceless, to the shores of death!

LVIII. — A TROUBLED SKY

It seems your eyes are covered by a hazy dew.
Your enigmatic eyes (are they green, grey or blue?)
Now tender, now reflective, now malevolent,
Reflect the lassitude of the pale firmament.

You bring to mind those days, warm, languid, and unclear,
That make enraptured hearts shed a reluctant tear,
When, shaken by a strange and ominous unrest,
Nerves that are too alert disturb the spirit's rest.

At times you are so like those charming horizons
Lit by the hazy suns of nebulous seasons…
Lustrous rain-washed landscapes, how resplendent you lie,
Lit by the sun's rays piercing a chaotic sky!

O dangerous woman, O fascinating climes,
Will I as well adore your blizzards and your rimes,
And in the cold, relentless winter, shall I feel
Delights more razor-sharp than ice or whetted steel?

LIX. — THE CAT

I

Within my fancy, on the prowl,
There goes a handsome, gentle cat,
As if he were in his own flat.
I scarcely hear his soft meowl,

His tone is so discreet and warm,
But whether waking or asleep,
His voice is always rich and deep:
There lies his secret and his charm.

That voice descends most dulcetly
My soul in pleasure to immerse,
Like a rhythmic, harmonious verse,
A philtre to enrapture me.

It calms the most distressing pain
And fills with joy my darkest days;
When uttering its longest phrase
No words are needed to explain.

No fiddler's bow could ever bring
More consonance into my heart
Or more concordant sounds impart
To its most vibrant, sweetest string,

Than your voice, cat of mystery,
O cat most strange and seraphic;
In whom all sounds are angelic,
So full of subtle harmony!

II

From his soft coat of black and white
There emanates such pleasant scent
That I was filled with sweet content
By stroking it, just once, one night.

The home is his familiar shrine,
He likes to judge, preside, inspire
All things that dwell in his empire;
Is he unworldly, or divine?

When to this cherished cat my eyes
Are drawn like magnets, then return
Within myself, I there discern,
To my most exquisite surprise,

The flame, the strange, exotic rays
Of his pale, opalescent eyes,
Clear beacons, luminescent, wise,
That fixedly return my gaze.

LX. – THE BEAUTIFUL SHIP

I want to tell you, gentle enchantress, the truth
Of all the many beauties that adorn your youth!
I want to show you your beauty,
Where youthfulness is allied to maturity.

When flouncing your wide skirts with such nobility,
You have the air of a fine ship that takes to sea,
Whose sails the zephyr breezes blow
Upon its rhythmic course, gentle, lazy, and slow.

Upon your ample shoulders and your shapely neck,
Your head parades its charms to singular effect.
With a most placid, noble air
You go upon your way, majestic child so fair.

I want to tell you, gentle enchantress, the truth
Of all the many beauties that adorn your youth!
I want to show you your beauty,
Where youthfulness is allied to maturity.

Against the silken moiré of your heaving breast,
Your comely bosom is a finely crafted chest
Of which the panels, curved and bright,
Like silver shields emblazon the reflected light.

Alluring shields, adorned with pointed rosy rings!
Casket of secrets sweet, replete with wondrous things,
Aromas, liquors, spices, wine,
That fill the heart and mind with transports so divine!

When flouncing your wide skirts with such nobility,
You have the air of a fine ship that takes to sea,
Whose sails the zephyr breezes blow
Upon its rhythmic course, gentle, lazy, and slow.

Your noble limbs, beneath the folds they cause to sway,
Give torment to the dark desires on which they prey,
Like sorceresses as they turn
The contents of a steaming potion in an urn.

Your arms, which could do sport with youthful Hercules,
Might be compared to glistening boas, as they squeeze
In a most obstinate caress
Your swain, as if his mark on your heart to impress.

Upon your ample shoulders and your shapely neck,
Your head parades its charms to singular effect.
With a most placid, noble air
You go upon your way, majestic child so fair.

LXI. — BERTHA'S EYES

You put the most illustrious eyes into the shade,
Fair eyes of my dear child, that filter to my sight
Things that are pure, serene, and gentle as the Night!
Fair eyes, bestow on me your charms that never fade!

Wide eyes of my dear child, arcana most adored,
You bear a great resemblance to those magic caves
In which, behind a cluster of lethargic shades,
There scintillate a host of treasures long ignored!

My child has eyes that are obscure, profound and vast
As you, colossal Darkness, monumental Night!
Their fires are thoughts of Love, mingled with Faith and Light,
That sparkle in their depths, voluptuous or chaste.

LXII. – THE FOUNTAIN

Your lovely eyes are tired, my sweet!
Sleep on in that unstudied guise,
So nonchalantly indiscreet,
Where pleasure took you by surprise.
The fountain burbles endlessly
Out in the courtyard, day and night,
Sustaining the sweet ecstasy
That love accorded me tonight.

There blossoms forth a spray
Of floral spheres,
Where Phoebe's bright display
Gaily appears,
And falls in an array
Of heavy tears.

And thus your ardent soul ignites
In hedonistic ecstasy,
And rushes boldly to the heights
Of the vast sky's infinity,
Until, expiring, losing hope,
In languid dole it falls apart,
Cascading down a hidden slope
Into the haven of my heart.

There blossoms forth a spray
Of floral spheres,
Where Phoebe's bright display
Gaily appears,
And falls in an array
Of heavy tears.

You whom the night doth render fair,
How sweet it is, upon your breast,
To hear, in the ethereal air,
The fountains sobbing without rest!
Moon, rippling water, blessed night,
Leaves whispering in the trees above,
The languor of your sweet delight
Is the reflection of my love.

There blossoms forth a spray
Of floral spheres,
Where Phoebe's bright display
Gaily appears,
And falls in an array
Of heavy tears.

LXIII. — INVITATION TO A JOURNEY

My sister, my heart,
How sweet to depart
To that faraway haven with you!
To languidly lie,
To love and to die
In a land that resembles you!
The damp suns that rise
In those nebulous skies
Seem to mirror the charm that appears
In the mystic disguise
Of your treacherous eyes,
Glistening through their tears.

There, all is order and beauty,
Luxury, calm and ecstasy.

Furnishings fine,
Embellished by time,
Would decorate our room;
And flowers most rare
Their fragrance would share
With amber's heady perfume,
Mirrors ornate,
And walls with the weight
Of Orient's splendour hung,
All things there would speak
In the secret mystique
Of their gentle native tongue.

There, all is order and beauty,
Luxury, calm, and ecstasy.

See those vessels that brave
The wind and the wave
Rocking gently in their berth;
It is to inspire
Your every desire
That they come from the ends of the earth.
— The sun goes down,
Setting the town,
The meadows and rivers alight
With jacinth and gold;
Our dreams unfold
In a gently warming light.

There, all is order and beauty,
Luxury, calm and ecstasy.

LXIV. — THE VOICE

My crib adjoined the library, when I was just
The size of a small folio. A sombre Babel,
Replete with Latin ashes and thick Grecian dust,
Enshrined many a tome of science, ode and fable.
Two voices spoke to me. One, firm and treacherous,
Said: "Earth is like a cake, and full of sweet surprise;
I can (and your delights would be continuous)
Give you an appetite to equal it in size."
The other said: "Come with me, rove with me in dreams,
Beyond the possible, beyond all that is known!"
And that voice sang like desert sands and mountain streams,
(Who knows from whence it came?) on phantom breezes blown,
Caressing awesomely the senses with its sound.
I answered: "Yes, most gentle voice!" And from that date,
Alas! I suffer from what could be called my wound
And my predestiny, forerunner of my fate.
Behind immense existence, in the vast abyss,
I clearly see strange worlds, fantastic and discrete,
And, victim of my clairvoyance, I hear the hiss
Of serpents that beset me, biting at my feet.
And it is since that time that, like prophets and seers,
I've loved devotedly the desert and the sea;
I've laughed at funerals, at parties I've shed tears,
And found a honeyed taste in wine's acerbity;
I often mistake falsehood for veracity,
And, eyes turned to the sky, I tumble into pits,
But then the voice consoles: "Pursue your reverie:
Wise men's dreams are no match for those of lunatics!"

LXV. — THE IRREPARABLE

Can we not suffocate the old, the long Remorse,
That lives, and writhes, and would us choke,
And feeds upon us like a worm upon a corpse,
A caterpillar on an oak?
Can we not suffocate implacable Remorse?

In what elixir, in what wine, in what tisane,
Shall we drown that old combatant,
As greedy and destructive as a courtesan,
As patient as a worker ant?
In what elixir? — in what wine? — in what tisane?

Tell me, fair sorceress, oh! tell me if you know,
Tell this soul that in dire remorse
Is like a dying soldier who has been laid low
And trampled by a passing horse,
Tell him, fair sorceress, oh! tell him if you know,

That dying man who senses the wolf's patient stare
And the eyes of the carrion crow;
That broken soldier, how he surely must despair
Of having a tomb here below!
That dying man who senses the wolf's patient stare!

Can we illuminate a dark and mournful sky?
Can this obscurity be torn
Apart, that is more dense than pitch, more black than dye,
With neither evening, nor morn?
Can we illuminate a dark and mournful sky?

The Hope that shines forth from the windows of the Inn
Is snuffed out, gone for evermore!
There is no moon to guide them and no light within
To bring lost martyrs to its door!
The Devil has blacked out the windows of the Inn!

Enchanting sorceress, say, do you love the damned?
Do you know the untenable?
Do you know of Remorse, with poison in its hand,
To which hearts are susceptible?
Entrancing sorceress, say, do you love the damned?

The Irreparable gnaws with its accursèd bite
Our soul, pitiful monument,
And often it attacks, like a malignant termite,
The building's very fundament.
The Irreparable gnaws with its accursèd bite!

— I've sometimes seen upon a banal stage appear,
To a roll of the timpani,
A fairy who ignites a dark celestial sphere
With wondrous luminosity;
I've sometimes seen upon a banal stage appear

A being, who was only radiance, gauze, and gold,
Bringing down Satan from his reign;
But my heart, that can never ecstasy behold,
Is a theatre where in vain
We wait to see that Being with her wings of gold!

LXVI. — CAUSERIE

You are a lovely autumn sky of limpid rose!
But melancholy rises in me like the sea,
And leaves, as it flows back, on lips sad and morose
The stinging memory of its acerbity.

— In vain you lay your hand upon my fainting breast;
The place it seeks, my darling, is now derelict,
By woman's teeth and claws ferociously possessed.
Seek then no more my heart; the beasts have eaten it.

My heart's a palace blighted by the rabble, where
They roister, pull each other's hair, sometimes they kill!
— Around your naked breast a perfume fills the air!...

O Beauty, cruel scourge of souls, it is your will!
With your bright eyes of fire, kindled as for a feast,
Incinerate these scraps left over by the beast!

LXVII. — AUTUMN SONG

I

Soon we shall all be plunged into the frozen gloom;
Farewell, resplendent days of summers all too short!
I can already hear, like an impending doom,
The firewood crashing down on the stones of the court.

Soon my soul will be gripped by winter's icy spell,
Beset by hatred, anger, horror, storm and flood,
And, like a sun imprisoned in its polar hell,
My wretched heart will be a block of ice and blood.

I shudder as I hear each timber as it falls;
The building of a scaffold echoes thus. I am
In spirit like a tower whose decaying walls
Succumb beneath the pounding of the battering ram.

That dull, relentless thud on me begins to pall,
Resounding like a hammer on a funeral bier.
For whom? - Lately was summer; now it is the fall!
I sense that a departure may be drawing near.

II

I love the emerald light that shines in your wide eyes,
Fair beauty, but today all things embitter me,
And nothing, not even the boudoir's sweet surprise,
Can match the shimmer of the sun upon the sea.

And yet, do love me, tender heart! Let your caress,
Even for an ingrate, even a wicked one,
Lover or sister, be the fleeting gentleness
Of autumn's transient glory or the setting sun.

Brief task! The tomb awaits, eager and appetent!
Ah! Let me taste, my brow reposing on your knee,
Lamenting the lost days of summer's torrid scent,
The gentle golden rays of autumn's clemency!

LXVIII. — TO A MADONNA
EX-VOTO IN THE SPANISH STYLE

I want to build for you, Madonna, mistress mine,
Deep in the depths of my despair, a secret shrine,
And in the very darkest corner of my heart,
Far from worldly desires and mocking eyes apart,
Carve out a niche, enamelled in both blue and gold,
In which will stand your Statue, wondrous to behold.
And with my polished Verse, lattice of metal fine,
Arranged most skilfully in stars of crystal rhyme,
I shall make for your head a massive Diadem,
And from my Jealousy I'll cut and sew the hem,
O mortal lady mine, of a Mantle designed
In stiff and heavy cloth, with deep suspicion lined,
A refuge for your charms, a haven for my fears,
Embroidered not with Pearls, but with my bitter Tears!
Your Robe will be composed of my intense Desire,
That rises, falls, and rises, trembles, rises higher,
Pulsating at the peaks, resting in the abyss,
And covering your body with an ardent kiss.
Of my Respect I'll make you Shoes of satin fine,
Which surely will be humbled by your feet divine,
And holding them within their soft embrace so warm,
Will keep the moulded imprint of their perfect form.
If I cannot, despite my diligence and skill,
Design a silver moon-shaped Pedestal, I will,
Instead, insert the Snake that gnaws me deep inside
Beneath your feet, that you may trample and deride,
Victorious Queen, redeemer of my anguished soul,
This monster swollen up with hate and bitter gall.
And you will see my Thoughts, like Candles all aligned
Before the Virgin's altar, all with flowers entwined,
Illumining with stars the vault of azure blue,
Their eyes of fire forever watching over you;
And as I hold for you such cherished thoughts within,
All will be Frankincense, Amber and Benjamin,
And ceaselessly toward your snow-white peak shall soar
My troubled Spirit, seeking all that I adore.

And finally, your role as Mary to perfect,
To mix barbarity with love and due respect,
Out of the seven Deadly Sins, O black delight!
I shall forge seven Knives, all sharp and burnished bright,
And then, with mingled nonchalance and self-disgust,
Taking your deepest love as target, I shall thrust
Each one of them in turn into your panting Heart,
Into your sobbing Heart, into your streaming Heart!

LXIX. — AFTERNOON SONG

Though your playful eyebrows rise
With a strangely wanton air
That an angel could not share,
Temptress with bewitching eyes,

I adore you fervently,
Frivolous and wayward love!
With the dedication of
Priests for their idolatry.

Desert breeze and woodland air
In your tresses waft and play,
And your mystic looks betray
Attitudes arcane and rare.

On your flesh sweet scents alight
As if from an incense urn;
Your enchantment long will burn
In my heart, tenebrous sprite.

Ah! no elixir can wed
Ardour with your languidness,
For you know the soft caress
That resuscitates the dead!

Your fine haunches complement
Your exquisite back and breast,
And, when languidly you rest,
Cushions revel in your scent.

On occasion, to requite
Your mysterious desire,
You will lavish all the fire
Of your kisses and your bite.

Dark one, your disdainful smile
Tears my very soul apart,
Then you place upon my heart
Gentle glances that beguile.

Neath the satin finery
Of your charming silken feet,
All my rapture I secrete,
My genius and destiny;

You, all colour and all light,
You have made my soul complete!
Explosion of summer's heat
In my dark Siberian night!

LXX. — SISINA

Imagine Diana, apparelled for the chase,
Roaming the forests, casting undergrowth aside,
Defiant, proud, breast bared, wind in her hair and face;
Her fleetness with the finest horsemen would have vied!

Or have you seen Theroigne, who loved the bloody fray,
Rousing the shoeless multitude to take a stand,
Her cheeks and eyes ablaze as she showed them the way,
Taking by storm the royal palace, sword in hand?

So too Sisina! But this gentle warrior shows
A nature that is kind as well as bellicose;
Her courage, bolstered up by drum and musket fire,

Can also lay down arms when it is met by fears
And supplications. Her heart has, though stirred by fire,
For those who merit grace, a reservoir of tears.

LXXI. — FRANCISCAE MEAE LAUDES

Novis te cantabo chordis,
O novelletum quod ludis
In solitudine cordis.

Esto sertis implicata,
Ô femina delicata
Per quam solvuntur peccata!

Sicut beneficum Lethe,
Hauriam oscula de te,
Quae imbuta es magnete.

Quum vitiorum tempestas
Turbabat omnes semitas,
Apparuisti, Deitas,

Velut stella salutaris
In naufragiis amaris...
Suspendam cor tuis aris!

Piscina plena virtutis,
Fons æternæ juventutis,
Labris vocem redde mutis!

Quod erat spurcum, cremasti;
Quod rudius, exaequasti;
Quod debile, confirmasti.

In fame mea taberna,
In nocte mea lucerna,
Recte me semper guberna.

Adde nunc vires viribus,
Dulce balneum suavibus
Unguentatum odoribus!

LXXI. — IN PRAISE OF MY FRANCESCA

I shall sing to you upon new chords
O child, as you play
In the solitude of my heart.

Be adorned with garlands,
O delightful woman
By whom sins are absolved!

As from a benevolent Lethe,
I shall drink kisses from you,
Who are imbued with magnetism.

When a tempest of vices
Invaded all my paths,
You appeared, Deity,

Like a star of salvation
To a disastrous shipwreck…
I shall hang my heart on your altars!

Lake full of virtue,
Fount of eternal youth,
Give back voice to my mute lips!

What was impure, you have burnt;
What was rough, you made smooth;
What was weak, you made strong.

In hunger you are my tavern,
In the night you are my lamp,
Guide me always on the right path.

Add now strength to my strength,
Sweet bath with pleasant
Odours scented!

Meos circa lumbos mica,
O castitatis lorica,
Aqua tincta seraphica;

Patera gemmis corusca,
Panis salsus, mollis esca,
Divinum vinum, Francisca!

Shine about my loins,
O belt of chastity,
Moistened with angelic water;

Bowl flashing with gemstones,
Salted bread, gourmet food,
Heavenly wine, Francesca!

LXXII. — TO A WOMAN OF MALABAR

Your hands and feet are slender, and your hips are quite
As generous as those of any buxom white;
Your silken flesh would be a thoughtful artist's prize,
And darker than your skin are your wide velvet eyes.

In sunlit azure lands where your God gave you birth,
You light the smoking-pipe of your master on earth,
You fill his bottles with cool water and perfume,
You banish mayflies and mosquitoes from his room,
And, when the plane-tree's song echoes the morning's call,
You buy figs and bananas from the market stall.
You wander barefoot where you fancy all day long,
Humming in dulcet tones an old mysterious song;
And when the dusk descends in its mantle of red,
You gently lay your body on a wicker bed,
Where, like your gracious self, your silent dreaming hours
Are filled with hummingbirds and subtly scented flowers.

Why, happy child, would you for France forsake this life,
That over-peopled land where suffering is rife,
And, trusting life and limb to sailors and the winds,
Bid last farewells to your beloved tamarinds?
Attired so meagrely in muslin thin and frail,
Aquiver there beneath the snowflakes and the hail,
How you would miss the gentle joys of bygone days
If, in a brutal prison of constricting stays,
You had to glean your supper in some sordid place
And sell the subtle perfume of your charming grace,
And follow scattered phantoms, with your pensive gaze,
Of absent palm trees in the filthy mist and haze!

LXXIII. — TO A CREOLE LADY

In a fair-perfumed land warmed by the sun's caress,
I met, 'neath swaying palms by zephyr breezes blown,
Where one may languish long in blissful idleness,
A Creole lady blest with charms to men unknown.

Her features pale yet warm, this dark-haired enchantress
Exhibits such a noble bearing in her gait;
Tall, stately, svelte, she has the air of a huntress;
Her smiling eyes betray a calm, untroubled state.

Were you to go, Madame, to glorious lands afar,
To the banks of the Seine or of the verdant Loire,
Your beauty, fit to grace an ancient country seat,

Would make the eager heart of every poet beat,
Inspire in them a thousand sonnets full of joy,
And make them more your slave than any servant boy.

LXXIV. — MŒSTA ET ERRABUNDA

Tell me, Agatha, does your heart not sometimes fly
Away, far from the city's dark, infested sea,
Toward another sea, beneath another sky,
As blue and clear and deep as pure virginity?
Tell me, Agatha, does not your heart sometimes fly?

The sea, the boundless sea, consoles our troubled mind!
What demon has bestowed upon the raucous sea,
That roars, accompanied by the discordant wind,
The faculty to soothe and calm adversity?
The sea, the boundless sea, consoles our troubled mind!

Carriage, carry me off! Vessel, take me away!
Far! Far! for here the earth is watered by our tears!
— Is it not true that Agatha's sad heart might say
Sometimes: Far from remorse, suffering, doubts and fears,
Carriage, carry me off! Vessel, take me away?

How far away you are, sweet-scented paradise,
Where under azure skies dwell love and harmony,
Where everything we love must unto love suffice,
Where every heart is bathed in purest ecstasy.
How far away you are, sweet-scented paradise!

But the green paradise of sweet precocious love,
Songs, kisses, country walks, bouquets of fragrant flowers,
With violins vibrating in the hills above,
And goblets full of wine by night in leafy bowers,
— But the green paradise of sweet precocious love,

Innocent paradise, full of clandestine charms,
Is it still farther off than China's Eastern main?
Can we recapture it, embrace it in our arms,
And with a silver voice bring it to life again,
Innocent paradise, full of clandestine charms?

LXXV. — THE GHOST

Wild-eyed, like an angel of doom,
I'll creep back softly to your room,
And there beside your bed alight
With the dark shadows of the night;

And on your lips I shall bestow
Kisses cold as the pale moon's glow,
And my caresses, in the gloom,
Will be like serpents round a tomb.

When livid morning shows its face,
You'll find I'm just an empty space,
Where cold will linger till the night.

While others show you tenderness,
I shall, upon your youthfulness,
Preside with a regime of fright.

LXXVI. — AUTUMN SONNET

They say to me, your eyes, with their translucent glaze:
"Tell me, strange paramour, what in me gives you joy?"
— Be gracious now, be still! All things my heart annoy,
Except the candour of the primal creature's gaze.

My heart will not disclose to you its secret hell,
You, whose hands are a cradle that lulls me to sleep;
Its legend, writ in flame, must its dark counsel keep;
I abhor passion, and thinking makes me unwell!

Let us love gently, for Eros in his retreat
Lies secretly in wait to draw his deadly bow.
I know the weapons that his ancient arsenals stow:

Crime, horror, lunacy! — O pallid marguerite!
Are you, like me, a sun with an autumnal glow,
O my so white, O my so frigid Marguerite?

LXXVII. — SORROWS OF THE MOON

Tonight, the moon is rapt in idle reverie;
Like an exquisite beauty, who in slumber rests
Upon a bed of cushions, fondling carelessly,
Before she falls asleep, the contour of her breasts,

Against an avalanche of satin and of silk,
Expiring, she gives way to swooning ecstasy,
And follows with her gaze the visions white as milk
That rise and flourish in the blue infinity.

When on occasion she lets fall upon this sphere,
In idle languidness, just one clandestine tear,
A pious poet, who in sleepless study lies,

In the palm of his hand takes that tear for his own,
That tear, reflecting like an opalescent stone,
And puts it in his heart far from the bright sun's eyes.

LXXVIII. — CATS

When ardent lovers and austere scholars grow old,
Both are inclined to love, in their maturity,
The powerful, gentle cat, pride of the family,
Who like them loves to sit, and like them shuns the cold.

Friends of both science and of sensuality,
Cats like to seek the silent horror of the dark;
As stallions of Erebus they'd have made their mark,
Had they to servitude inclined their dignity.

As they dream, they adopt the noble attitude
Of the great sphinx, recumbent in deep solitude,
Seeming to dream forever in its desert land;

From their abundant loins magical sparks arise,
And particles of gold, like grains of finest sand,
Confusedly bestar their enigmatic eyes.

LXXIX. — THE OWLS

Beneath the shade of black yew trees,
Like strange, exotic deities,
With piercing eyes, in solemn state,
The owls sit. They meditate.

There, motionless, they will remain
Until the sun goes down again,
That strangely melancholic hour
When darkness shrouds the leafy bower.

Their attitude teaches the wise
To shun all movement and surprise
And to eschew life's daily race;

The man who follows every whim
Will find that life will punish him
For always wanting to change place.

LXXX. — THE PIPE

I am an author's pipe; you'll see,
When you observe my dusky mien
Of Abyssinian or Cafrine,
That he must smoke most heavily.

When he is burdened by concern,
I smoke like an old chimney hood,
Where dishes filled with steaming food
Await the ploughman's safe return.

I cradle and enlace his soul
Within the opalescent veil
That rises in a swirling trail

Of potent spices from my bowl,
To charm his heart and rid his mind
Of all the troubles it might find.

LXXXI. — MUSIC

Music often uplifts me like an endless sea!
Toward my pale star,
Beneath an azure dome or misty canopy,
I set sail afar;

Breast to the fore and lungs swollen with salted air
Like a canvas sail,
I scale the contours of the surging billows where
Night has cast its veil;

I feel vibrating in me all the emotions
Of a suffering ship;
The fair wind, or the storm and its convulsions

On the boundless deep
Lull me. Or else dead calm, like a great mirror there,
Reflecting my despair!

LXXXII. — SEPULCHRE

If on a dank and dismal night
A good soul, out of charity,
Should bury somewhere, out of sight,
Your once proud body, secretly,

When daylight wanes and moonlight ebbs
And stars are sleeping peacefully,
The spiders there will spin their webs,
And vipers hatch their progeny;

And every day throughout the year
Above your damned head you will hear
The wolf's pathetic, plaintive howl,

Gaunt witches chanting sorcery,
Old men sating their lechery
And villains plotting deeds most foul.

LXXXIII. — A FANTASTIC ENGRAVING

As sole attire, this spectre risen from the dead
Has, balancing grotesquely on his bony head,
A hideous diadem, like something from a fair.
Devoid of whip or spur, he rides a flagging mare,
A phantom just like him, apocalyptic nag,
Whose nostrils drip with foam like some convulsive hag.
The two of them press on regardless into space,
Trampling infinity in their audacious race.
The horseman holds aloft an incandescent sword,
Which flashes as his mount fragments the nameless horde,
And, like a prince who scans his realm, he casts his eye
About the cold, unbounded graveyard in which lie,
Lit by a lifeless sun's obscure translucency,
The peoples of antique and modern history.

LXXXIV. — THE HAPPY CORPSE

In a rich, fertile soil where snails live at their ease,
I want to dig a deep and spacious cavity,
Where I can idly stretch my old bones as I please
And sleep, oblivious, like a shark in the sea.

I have no time for tombs or wills in wordy prose,
And rather than implore the world its tears to share,
While I still live, I would prefer to ask the crows
To feed upon my blood and strip my carcass bare.

O worms! companions dark, with neither eye nor ear,
Behold my free, contented corpse as I draw near;
Debauched philosophers, foul offspring of decay,

Feel free to take this ruin for your daily bread,
And if you know of further torments, tell me, pray,
For this old soulless body, dead among the dead!

LXXXV. — THE CASK OF HATRED

Hatred is like the cask of the pale Danaïdes;
Bewildered Vengeance with her arms so strong and red
In vain its dark recesses from her ewer feeds
With blood and tears from all the legions of the dead,

The Fiend in its abyss has hidden secret holes,
Through which escape a thousand years of sweat and strain,
But even so, she could reanimate their souls,
And resurrect their corpse to squeeze them dry again.

Hatred is like a drunken man in a taverna,
Who feels his thirst reborn with every draught of liquor
And reproduce itself like the Hydra of Lerna.

— But some fortunate drinkers know their conqueror,
And Hatred's sad misfortune is to be unable
To learn the art of sleeping underneath the table.

LXXXVI. – THE ABYSS

Pascal had his abyss that followed him each day.
— Alas! All is abyss, — desire, word, action, dream!
And in my hair that stands straight up on end, I seem
To often feel the wind of Fear along the way.

Above, below, on every side, the depth, the strand,
The silence, the horrendous, captivating space…
Upon the canvas of my nights God's fingers trace
A complex, endless nightmare with a knowing hand.

I am afraid of sleep, as one might fear a hole
That's full of obscure horrors, leading to no goal;
Each window shows me nothing but infinity,

And my sad spirit, racked by instability,
Is envious of the void's insensibility.
— From Entities and Numbers never to be free!

LXXXVII. — THE CRACKED BELL

It is so bittersweet, on a long winter's night,
To listen, as the fire logs crackle in my room,
To distant memories that gradually alight,
As pealing carillons ring out across the gloom.

That venerable bell with its vigorous throat,
Which, notwithstanding age, is active and content,
Emitting faithfully its clear religious note,
Like an old soldier keeping watch inside his tent!

My soul is a cracked bell, and when in its ennui
It wants to fill the night air with its melody,
It sometimes happens that its feeble moaning can

Seem like the choking rattle of a wounded man,
Who, in a pool of blood, inhales his dying breath
And struggles, motionless, beneath a mound of death.

LXXXVIII. — SPLEEN I

Pluviose, venting his ire on the community,
Pours from his urn great floods of winter's elements
On the pale inmates of the nearby cemetery
And death upon the gloomy town's inhabitants.

My cat upon the flagstones seeks to make his bed,
Shaking incessantly his body, gaunt and old,
And in the drains there roams a poet long since dead,
Whose melancholy accents tremble in the cold.

The bell sounds its lament, and the spluttering log
Joins in falsetto with the wheezing of the clock,
While in a deck of cards that reeks with rancid scent,

Fatal endowment of a dropsical old maid,
The handsome knave of hearts and the old queen of spades
Discuss in eerie tones their passions long since spent.

LXXXIX. — SPLEEN II

I have more memories than if I'd lived a thousand years.

A bulky chest of drawers replete with souvenirs,
Love letters, poems, books, receipts, lawsuits and wills,
And heavy locks of hair wrapped up in faded bills,
Would harbour fewer secrets than my troubled head.
It is a pyramid, a grotto for the dead
That holds more corpses than the great communal tomb.
— I am a graveyard that's detested by the moon,
Where, like some dire remorse, a veritable host
Of worms devour the flesh of those I loved the most.
I am an old boudoir replete with wilted blooms,
In which there lies a pile of outmoded costumes,
Where pale Bouchers and drawings in the pastel style
Alone inhale the odours from an open vial.

Nothing can match in length those limping, dreary days,
When, weighed down by the years of winter's icy glaze,
Ennui, the fruit of our incuriosity,
Takes on the amplitude of immortality.
— Henceforth you are no more, O living entities!
Than granite blocks surrounded by a dread unease,
Slumbering in the depths of a Saharan haze;
An ancient sphinx, unknown to these uncaring days,
Forgotten on the map, whose enigmatic gaze
Speaks only to the setting sun's declining rays.

XC. — SPLEEN III

I'm like a king who rules a land that's wet and cold,
Wealthy but powerless, youthful but very old,
Who scorns the flattery of his obsequious teachers,
Preferring to be bored by dogs and other creatures.
Nothing can stir him, neither hunt nor falconry,
Nor even starving serfs beneath his balcony.
His jester's grotesque stories, told in rhyme or prose,
No longer can relieve this morbid patient's woes;
His bed, adorned with fleurs-de-lys, becomes a tomb;
Even the lovely ladies of the court, for whom
All princes have allure, can find no robe to don
That could evince a smile from this young skeleton.
The alchemist who makes his gold cannot invent
A method to extract the corrupt element
From him, and in those bloodbaths ancient Romans knew,
Which in their dotage powerful men recall anew,
He could not warm the heart of this corpse dull and grey,
Where flows not blood, but water from the green Lethe.

XCI. — SPLEEN IV

When the low, heavy sky weighs down like a great lid
Upon the plaintive heart that's prey to long ennui,
Embracing the horizon's great circular grid,
Bringing days more morose than night's obscurity;

When earth has been transformed into a dripping cell,
Where Hope, like an unseeing bat, lost and alone,
Instinctively pursues its reckless course pell-mell,
Striking its head and wings against the crumbling stone;

When the vertical lances of the falling rain
Resemble prison bars behind which our life ebbs,
And stretching wide their network deep inside our brain,
A vast army of spiders comes to spin its webs,

Bells spring to life abruptly and ferociously,
Sending toward the sky their loud and fearsome sound,
Like homeless souls that rise and wander aimlessly,
Weeping and wailing as they drag themselves around.

— And a cortège of hearses, slowly, silently,
Meanders through my soul, where vanquished Hope is dead;
While Anguish, cruel despot, plants triumphantly
His evil standard on my subjugated head.

XCII. — THE UNFORESEEN

Harpagon, keeping vigil at his father's bed,
Seeing the lips already pale, began to muse:
"I think we must have ample stock there in the shed
Of old boards that we could still use?"

A cooing Célimène declares: "My heart is good,
And God has given me beauty that men proclaim."
— Her heart! a shrivelled heart, a ham smoked over wood,
And cooked by the eternal flame!

A feeble hack, who thinks that he's a shining light,
Says to the wretch he's drowned in a tenebrous mere:
"Where do you see this architect of Truth and Right,
This great Avenger you revere?"

Better than all of these, I know a debauchee
Who night and day laments and weeps in doleful sorrow,
Repeating, feeble blockhead: "Just you wait and see,
I shall be virtuous come tomorrow!"

The clock in turn confides: "He's ready for the call,
The damned one! For I have in vain warned of his flaws.
Man is both deaf and blind, and fragile as a wall
In which an insect lives and gnaws!"

And then, Someone appears, whom all had long denied,
Who proudly taunts them, saying: "I have seen you pass
Before me in the proud communion I provide
So joyously at the Black Mass.

You each build in your heart a temple to my name;
Each of you has in secret kissed my foul behind!
Acknowledge Satan and his ever-conquering fame,
As monstrous as the world is blind!

Did you think, hypocrites whom my presence surprises,
That you could mock and cheat your lord without a hitch,
That it could be your lot to win both of the prizes,
To go to Heaven *and* be rich?"

The game must pay the hunter who has stalked his prey
And lain so long in wait, perfecting his decoy.
Now through the thickness I shall carry you away,
Companions of my sombre joy,

Down through the thickness of the ancient soil and rock,
The tangled remnants of your ashes and your bone,
Into a palace built, like me, of one great block,
And which is not of tender stone;

For it is wholly made of universal Sin,
And harbours all my pride, my pain and majesty!"
— However, high above the realms of worldly sin
An angel sounds the victory

Of those whose hearts can say: "May your scourge give us joy,
O Lord! and all our sorrows, Father, may you bless!
My spirit, in your hands, is not a useless toy,
And your wisdom is measureless."

The trumpet's sound is so delightful as it flows,
Flooding celestial harvests with its solemn lays,
That it imbues with ecstasy the souls of those
Of whom it sings the fervent praise.

XCIII. — THE LAMENTS OF AN ICARUS

Lovers of whores are never cowed,
They're satisfied and well-content;
But as for me, my arms are spent
For having tried to hug a cloud.

Thanks to the stars, the peerless ones,
That in the boundless heavens shine,
My burnt-out eyes can only find
The memories of smouldering suns.

In vain I've tried to find the end
And the dividing line of space,
But in some incandescent place
I feel my melting pinions bend;

The love of beauty was my doom:
I'll never know the noble bliss
Of being named in the abyss
Which will serve as my final tomb.

XCIV. — OBSESSION

Great forests, like cathedrals you fill me with dread;
Your roar is like an organ; in our blighted soul,
Chamber of endless grief and moaning of the dead,
Of your *De Profundis* the mournful echoes roll.

Ocean of my despair! Your tumult and your swell
Wound me! The bitter laugh, the animosity
Of vanquished man, his curses and his tears that well,
I hear them in the monstrous laughter of the sea.

How pleasant you would be without your stars, O night!
The language that they speak is too well-known to me!
Darkness and emptiness are all I want to see!

But even emptiness and darkness, to my sight,
Are canvases where live the souls of bygone days,
Whose eyes encounter mine with their familiar gaze.

XCV. — A TASTE FOR THE VOID

Sad spirit, erstwhile so enamoured of the fray,
Hope, whose keen spur was wont to make you run and leap,
No longer wants to mount you! Lie now down to sleep,
Old horse who trips and stumbles all along the way.

Resign yourself, my heart, and sleep your cares away.

Defeated, worn-out soul, who knew the brigand's art!
There's no more joy in love, nor pleasure in dispute;
Farewell then, songs of brass and sighing of the flute!
O Pleasures, tempt no more this gloomy, pining heart!

Sweet Spring no longer can her fragrances impart!

And Time enshrouds my life in its relentless pall,
A snowdrift that engulfs a body stiff with cold;
— I look down from above, earth's roundness to behold,
But shelter there no longer beckons with its call.

Avalanche, will you take me with you in your fall?

XCVI. — ALCHEMY OF SORROW

One lights you, Nature, with its ardour,
The other casts you into gloom!
What says to one: I am your Doom!
Says to the other: Life and splendour!

Mystical Hermes who assist
Me, you who fill my heart with fear,
Of Midas you make me the peer,
That most unhappy alchemist;

I change, by your mysterious spell,
Gold into iron, heaven to hell;
I find, enshrouded in the sky,

A dear cadaver I knew well,
And on the shores of heaven I
Build towering sarcophagi.

XCVII. — CONGENIAL HORROR

From this bizarre and livid sky,
Tormented like your destiny,
What thoughts to your bereft soul fly?
Reply, wanton voluptuary.

— Ceaselessly, avidly, I seek
All that's obscure and imprecise:
I shall not borrow Ovid's pique,
Chased from his Latin paradise.

O skies chaotic as the sea,
In you is mirrored all my pride;
Your vast funereal clouds provide

The hearses of my fantasy,
And you reflect the living Hell
Wherein my heart is pleased to dwell.

XCVIII. — THE LID

Wherever he might go, on ocean or on land,
Beneath a fiery sky or an insipid sun,
Servant of Jesus Christ, Cythera's sycophant,
Beggar of dismal mien, Croesus the wealthy one,

Town-dweller, countryman, vagabond, sedentary,
Whether his little brain be resolute or shy,
Everywhere Man endures the dread of mystery,
And only looks above with trembling in his eye.

Above, the Sky! That suffocating tomb-like wall,
That ceiling lit up like a bawdy music-hall
Where on the blood-soaked floor clowns strut their vanity;

The lecher's dread unease, the crazy hermit's dream,
The Sky! Black lid of the great cauldron in which steam
The invisible hordes of vast Humanity.

XCIX. — THE SELF-TORMENTED

I'll strike you without rage or hate,
The way a butcher strikes the block,
The way that Moses struck the rock!
And from your eyes I'll irrigate,

With waters of your cares and fears,
My dry Sahara's searing fire.
Bolstered by hope, all my desire
Will float upon your salten tears

Like a vessel that puts to sea,
And in my heart, which they will fill
With drunkenness, your dear sobs will
Resound like charging cavalry!

Am I not a discordant strain
In the celestial symphony,
Thanks to voracious Irony
That shakes me, bites me, gives me pain?

She's in my voice, that screaming elf!
It's in my blood, this black morass!
I am the evil looking glass
Where the virago preens herself.

I am both wound and scimitar!
I am the cheek, I am the slap!
I am the body and the rack,
The victim and the torturer!

I suck my heart's blood willingly,
I'm one of those whom all revile
Who, though they can no longer smile,
Are doomed to laugh eternally.

C. — THE IRREMEDIABLE

I

A Being, an Idea, a Thought
That left the azure sky and fell
Into a Styx as dark as hell
That no celestial eye has sought;

An Angel, heedless voyager
Drawn by a love of hideous things,
Caught in a nightmare, beats his wings
And struggles like a spent swimmer,

O torment of impending doom!
Against the eddy's ruthless pull
That sings like some demented fool,
Gyrating in the dreadful gloom.

Wretched victim of sorcery,
He seeks in vain to break the spell
And flee from where vile reptiles dwell,
Seeking the daylight and the key;

A blighted soul who must descend
Into a dark abyss whose smell
Is redolent of a deep well,
Down railless stairways with no end,

Where slimy monsters gawp and gape
With eyes of phosphorus that glow,
And in the pitch-black darkness show
The horror of their loathsome shape;

A ship caught in a polar cell
Like some enormous crystal trap,
Seeking to find by what mishap
It came into this frozen hell;

— Clear metaphors that well portray
Irreparable destiny,
And illustrate the artistry
Of Satan's work in every way!

II

A tête-à-tête obscure yet clear,
A heart become its looking-glass!
Bright well of Truth and black morass
Where palpitates a livid star,

Infernal beacon, casting wide
The irony of Satan's grace,
Singular glory and solace,
  — Conscious Evil personified!

CI. — "TASSO IN PRISON" BY EUGÈNE DELACROIX

The poet in his cell, ailing and desolate,
Rolling a manuscript beneath his trembling foot,
Observes, consumed by all that he most apprehends,
The yawning chasm into which his soul descends.

The strident cries of mirth that in the jail are heard
Invite his reason to the strange and the absurd;
He is beset by Doubt; and Fear, ridiculous,
Around him circulates, diverse and hideous.

That intellect imprisoned in a stinking cell,
Those grimaces, those cries, those ghosts that swarm and swell,
Ferment and congregate behind his troubled ear,

This dreamer whose abode awakes in him such fear:
Such is your emblem, Soul whose dark dreams know no pause,
Stifled and choked within Reality's four walls.

CII. — THE PORTENDER

Any man fit to be so called
Has in his heart a snake-like Foe,
As if upon a throne installed;
If he says: "I will", Fang says "No!"

Plunge your eyes into the fixed gaze
Of Water Sprites or Satyr Maids,
Fang says: "Think Duty, not delight!"

Beget a child, or plant a tree,
Sculpt marble, polish poetry,
Fang says: "Will you still live tonight?"

Whatever plans he hopes to make,
Man cannot in this life forestall
The ever-present warning call
Of the intolerable Snake.

CIII. — THE MIDNIGHT REVIEW

The clock, sounding the midnight tone,
With irony engages us
Within our conscience to discuss
How we have used the day that's flown:
— Today, a most portentous date,
Friday the thirteenth, we have been,
Despite all we have known and seen,
Behaving like an apostate.

We have defiled the name of Jesus,
Of all the Gods the highest priest,
Like fawning leeches at the feast
Of some abominable Croesus;
To satisfy the brutish boor,
Worthy disciple of the Fiend,
All that we love we have demeaned
And glorified what we deplore.

Base torturers, we have oppressed
The weak, whom we wrongly disdain,
Given Stupidity free rein
With bovine single-mindedness;
Kissed banal Matter's foolishness
With the utmost devotion,
And of foul putrefaction
We've sanctified the bloodlessness.

And finally, to drown our dread
In transports of delirious fire,
We have, vain preachers of the Lyre,
Whose only glory is to spread
The rapture of funereal doom,
Dined without thirst or appetite!...
— Quickly, let us snuff out the light
And hide in the tenebrous gloom.

CIV. — THE CLOCK

O Clock! Sinister god, impassive, menacing,
Whose finger threatens us and tells us: "*Don't forget!*
Pulsating Torments will your trembling heart beset
And like the bowman's shaft will plant themselves therein.

Vaporous Pleasure to the horizon will flee
Just as a sylph into the wings might take her flight;
Each moment will devour a part of the delight
That each man in his lifetime is allowed to see.

Three thousand and six hundred times in every hour
The Second hand is heard to whisper: *Don't forget!*
— With his insect-like voice, Now quickly says: And yet,
I am the Past; I've sucked your lifeblood with my power!

Remember! Souviens-toi, wastrel! *Esto memor!*
(My metal larynx speaks these words in every tongue.)
Those minutes, fickle mortal, are gangues from which is wrung
The gold that is extracted from the precious ore!

Do not forget that avid Time has aces high
In every game, without deceit! — it is so writ.
The daylight wanes; the night augments; *remember it!*
The abyss always thirsts; the clepsydra is dry.

Shortly will sound the hour when transcendental Fate,
When Virtue most august, your still unsullied spouse,
When even Penitence (your ultimate safe house!)
When all will tell you: Die, old coward! It's too late!"

PARISIAN SCENES

CV. — LANDSCAPE

I wish, to write my eclogues in the purest verse,
To sleep close to the sky, like the astrologers,
And, as I dream, to listen to the solemn hymns
From nearby belfries that are borne upon the wind.
My chin cupped in my hands, there in my attic room,
I'll see the workshops, hear their banter and their tune,
The chimney pipes, the belfries, masts of the city,
And great skies that inspire dreams of eternity.

Lights in the windows, stars in the blue firmament
Across the evening haze, visions of pure content,
Rivers of smoke that rise toward the distant sky,
As the pale moon imparts its magic from on high.
I shall see springtime, summer, autumn's golden glow,
And when the winter comes with its relentless snow,
I shall close all the doors and shutters firm and tight
To build imaginary castles in the night.
And I shall dream of far horizons in the blue,
Of fountains weeping tears of alabaster hue,
Of ardent kisses and of birds that daylong sing,
Of all that makes the Idyll such a childlike thing.
The Riot, beating vainly at my window pane,
Will not cause me from my endeavours to refrain;
For I shall be engrossed in the voluptuous sight
Of Spring, whose pleasures I evoke with such delight,
And in the task of drawing from my heart with care
The sun that to my thoughts imparts its warming air.

CVI. — THE SUN

Along the run-down streets, where shuttered windows hide
The secret lecheries of those who dwell inside,
When the unyielding sun relentlessly beats down
Upon the fields of corn, the rooftops and the town,
I go to practice my strange swordplay on my own,
Seeking in every corner rhymes as yet unknown,
Tripping upon the words that I seek for my song,
Or stumbling upon verses dreamed of for so long.

This foster father, foe of all infirmity,
In rose and worm alike awakens poetry;
He turns our cares to vapour in the distant skies,
And fills our brains with honey from abundant hives.
He renders youthful those who walk with stick and crutch
And makes them gay of spirit and gentle of touch,
Enjoining all the crops to ripen and to nourish
The ever-beating heart that always strives to flourish!

When, like a poet, he descends into the town,
He renders noble all that's tawdry and run-down,
And, king-like, permeates, with great simplicity,
Dwellings and hospices with luminosity.

CVII. — TO A BEGGAR-GIRL

Sallow girl with russet hair,
Tatters in the clothes you wear
Show us both your poverty
And your beauty.

To a sickly bard like me,
Your young body's frailty,
With red freckles on your arms,
Still has its charms.

You wear far more gracefully
Than a queen of fantasy
Her buskins of velvet could,
Your clogs of wood.

Rather than a ragged dress,
Let a robe of great finesse
Trail its long and bustling pleats
About your feet;

And, instead of threadbare hose,
Where the roué's eyes repose
Let your noble thigh parade
A golden blade;

Let your loosely fastened bows
For our sins to us disclose
Your fair breast, whose beauty vies
With your bright eyes;

May your arms require a prayer
To remove the clothes you wear,
And may they firmly repel
Hands that rebel.

Pearls of opalescent glow,
Sonnets of master Belleau,
Offered to you by the swains
You keep in chains.

Rhymesters of the lowest art
Would to you their verse impart
When they see your slipper there
Beneath the stair.

Many a page would seek reward,
Many a Ronsard, many a lord
Would for favours gladly grovel
In your hovel!

You could take into your bed
Many an ardent noble head,
And under your sway could bring
More than one King.

— Yet you are condemned to eat
Scraps of bread and tainted meat
That someone has thrown away
Near some cafe;

And you covet secretly
Some cheap piece of jewellery,
But even such scant reward
I can't afford!

Go then with no ornament,
Perfume or accoutrement,
Other than your nudity,
O my beauty!

CVIII. — THE SWAN

To Victor Hugo

I

Andromache, I think of you! This little stream,
This melancholy mirror, which in bygone years
Shone with the majesty of a proud widow's dream,
This pseudo Simoeis that's swollen by your tears,

Rekindled suddenly my fertile memory,
As I was crossing the new Place du Carrousel.
Old Paris is no more (the shape of a city
Changes faster, alas! than mortals can foretell);

I see in my mind's eye where kiosks once had been,
Assorted pilasters and rough-hewn pediments,
Weeds, grasses, massive blocks that puddles had stained green,
And, gleaming in the windows, cluttered ornaments.

Once, a menagerie had been erected there;
Early one morning when, beneath cold, limpid skies,
The sound of refuse workers broke the silent air
With noisy shouts and carts, there came before my eyes

A swan that had escaped from its imprisonment,
And, on the dusty flagstones dragging its webbed feet,
Was trailing its white plumage on the rough pavement.
Beside a dried-up stream the bird opened its beak,

As nervously it tried to bathe its wings in soil,
And cried out, longing for the lake where it was born:
"Water, when will you fall? Thunder, when will you roll?"
Sometimes I see that swan, strange vision so forlorn,

Its head turned skyward like the man in Ovid's verse,
Toward the cruel irony of that blue sky,
Stretching convulsively its neck in dreadful thirst,
As if it to send admonishment to God on high.

II

Paris is changing! But in my melancholy
Nothing has moved! New palaces, scaffoldings, blocks,
Old suburbs, all for me becomes an allegory,
And all my memories weigh heavier than rocks.

And when before the Louvre I pause to pass the time,
The image of that great white swan haunts me anew,
Its desperate convulsions, grotesque and yet sublime,
The fruit of vain desire! And then I think of you,

Andromache, deprived of your husband's embrace,
Like a base chattel offered to a proud Pyrrhus,
Above an empty tomb inclined in solemn grace,
Hector's widow, alas! and wife of Helenus!

I call to mind a negress, phthisic, skin and bone,
Trudging through muddy streets, her eyes seeking in vain
The great coconut palms of her African home
Behind a massive, opaque wall of mist and rain;

All those who have now lost what they will never find
Again, never again! all those who drink their tears
And feed at Sorrow's breast, that she-wolf good and kind!
The orphans who like flowers wither with the years!

Thus, in the forest where my spirit is exiled,
A hunting horn resounds with memories anew!
I think of mariners forgotten on some isle,
Of prisoners and slaves!... and many others too!

CIX. — THE SEVEN OLD MEN

To Victor Hugo

Teeming, swarming city, city full of dreams,
Where even in broad daylight anyone might meet
A spectre! Mystery, flowing like nectar, seems
To fill the pipes and conduits of each narrow street.

One morning, in the dismal street, the sombre rank
Of houses seemed to rise up higher in the gloom,
As if they stood upon a swollen river's bank,
And, as a décor to reflect my thoughts of doom,

A filthy yellow fog just hung there like a pall.
Steeling my nerves as if to play a hero's part,
And arguing with my already weary soul,
I made my way to the sound of a rumbling cart.

Suddenly an old man emerged out of the mist,
In rags whose colour matched that of the sombre skies,
And whose aspect would have attracted alms and gifts,
But for the wickedness that glistened in his eyes

That looked as if they might have been immersed in gall,
Staring as if they could sharpen the winter's chill;
And his long shaggy beard projected from his jaw,
As Judas's beard might if he were living still.

He was not bent, but broken, and his level spine
Made with his lower half a right angle so straight
And perfect, that his cane, completing the design,
Lent him the strange appearance and the clumsy gait

Of a three-legged Jew or a lame quadruped.
Onward through mud and snow this apparition went,
As if under his shoes he were crushing the dead,
And he seemed hostile rather than indifferent.

Behind him came his double: eyes, back, stick, rags, beard,
No feature to distinguish this decrepit friend,
Offspring of the same hell, those apparitions weird
Advanced at the same pace toward some unknown end.

Of what infamous plot had I become the aim,
Or what harsh chance had come to humiliate me?
For I saw seven of him, and each one looked the same:
That sinister old man was cloning rapidly!

May he who laughs aloud at my anxiety,
Who does not nurture some fraternal sympathy,
Reflect that, notwithstanding their infirmity,
Those monsters had a semblance of eternity!

Could I have seen the eighth and yet still not succumb,
Inexorable double, fatal irony,
Appalling Phoenix, one his father, one his son?
— But I had turned my back on this vile parody.

Exasperated, like a drunkard seeing double,
I went home, locked the door, gripped by anxiety,
Confused and feverish, my spirit deeply troubled
By both the mystery and the absurdity!

In vain my reason tried to keep an even keel;
The tempest thwarted all its efforts scornfully;
Like an old raft, my soul could only dance and reel,
With neither mast nor sail, upon a shoreless sea.

CX. — THE LITTLE OLD WOMEN

To Victor Hugo

I

In any capital's sinuous maze of streets,
Where even horror can enchant in its own way,
I watch, in deference to my fatal conceits,
As strange, decrepit beings go about their day.

These shambling ruins once were women in their prime,
Eponine or Laïs! Now twisted, bent, forlorn;
But love them! for their spirit does not change with time.
In flimsy petticoats of cotton, frayed and torn,

They make their way, lashed by the north wind's cruel bite,
The clanking of the omnibus making them cower
In fright, and, like some precious relic, clutching tight
A little bag bearing a rebus or a flower.

Looking for all the world like little marionettes,
They trot along, or drag themselves like wounded beasts,
Or dance unwittingly, pathetic silhouettes,
Controlled by a malignant entity that feasts

Upon their frailty! Yet their eyes are sharp as drills,
And glow like little pools of water in the night,
Like the eyes of a child who innocently thrills
And laughs aloud at all that sparkles in the light.

— Do you know that the coffin of an ancient dame
Is often just as small as that of a small child?
All-knowing Death has made these coffins look the same,
A symbol most bizarre by which we are beguiled.

And when in teeming Paris I see one of those
Debilitated phantoms passing by, forlorn,
It seems to me that this frail being gently goes
Toward another crib in which to be reborn;

Unless, to pure geometry giving more thought,
Seeing those diverse limbs of every shape and size,
I ask myself how many times craftsmen have sought
To modify the box in which each body lies.

— Those eyes are like deep wells filled with a million tears,
Crucibles that are sequined by the cooling ore...
Those eyes of mystery are fascinating spheres
For those whom harsh Misfortune suckled with her lore!

II

Priestess of Vesta so in love with Frascati;
Priestess of Thalia, alas! whose very name
Only the prompter knows; vanished celebrity
Upon whom Tivoli once lavished such acclaim,

They all beguile me; but among those frail beings
There are some who know how to sublimate their pain,
And call upon Devotion to afford them wings:
Great Hippogriff, deliver me to Heaven's domain!

One, whose own country gave her grief and misery,
Another, whose own husband blighted her best years,
Or a Madonna, pierced by her own progeny,
Each of them could have made a river from her tears!

III

So many have I followed, time and time again!
One of them, when the setting sun's flamboyant arc
Imbued the evening sky with a vermilion stain,
Sat pensive, all alone, on a bench in a park,

To listen to the sound of trumpets and trombones,
One of those concerts often heard in public parks,
Given by army bands, whose rich and brassy tones
Inspire heroic thoughts within the townsmen's hearts.

She sat, proud and erect, as they began to play,
Intently savouring the grandiose parade;
Sometimes her eye would stare like an old bird of prey;
Her alabaster brow seemed for the laurel made!

IV

And so you make your way, stoic, without complaint,
As you traverse the chaos of the living town,
A mother sad of heart, a courtesan, a saint,
Names once revered by all, so great was your renown.

You who once knew such grace, you who such glory knew,
Now recognized by no-one! An ill-mannered drunk
Makes a contemptuous comment as he passes you,
While on your heels cavorts some vulgar, craven punk.

Ashamed to be alive, your wizened shadows stay
Close to the walls, backs bent, advancing timidly;
And no-one greets you as you go upon your way,
Debris of womankind ripe for eternity!

But I who from afar look on with tenderness
At your uncertain steps, your harsh and cruel plight,
As if I were your father, O what happiness!
Unknown to you I feel a clandestine delight:

I see your early passions coming into bloom;
Your vanished days, some sombre, others filled with light;
Your sins relieve my heart of its despairing gloom!
And in your virtues my resplendent soul glows bright!

Poor wrecks! My kindred spirits! My own family!
Each night I bid a solemn farewell to you all!
Where will you be tomorrow, octogenarian Eves,
Upon whom weighs the dread of God's relentless claw?

CXI. — THE BLIND

Just look at them, my soul; they are a dreadful sight!
Like weird automatons; vaguely ridiculous;
Absurd somnambulists, bizarre, preposterous,
Darting we know not where their eyes bereft of light.

Tenebrous eyes, from which the divine spark has fled,
As if their gaze were to the distant heavens bound;
They seem forever loath to turn toward the ground,
In peaceful reverie, their weary, troubled head.

Thus they traverse in darkness night's infinity,
That brother of eternal silence. O city!
While we can hear your laughter and your strident cry,

Your worship of indulgence, your atrocious game,
See! I trudge onward too! but, more confused than them,
I say: What do those blind men seek there in the Sky?

CXII. — TO A PASSER-BY

About me roared the noise and clamour of the town.
A widow, new-bereaved, tall, slender, stately, grand,
Passed by, and with a florid gesture of her hand,
Lifted and flounced the scalloped border of her gown.

Enchanted by her grace, her perfect symmetry,
Delirious, I drank, enraptured yet forlorn,
From her eyes, livid skies where hurricanes are born,
The sweetness that enthrals, the lethal ecstasy.

A lightning flash… then night! — O fugitive beauty
Whose transitory glance kindled new life in me,
Shall I see you again but in eternity?

Elsewhere, so far from here! Too late! *Never*, maybe?
For I know not your fate, nor you my destiny,
You whom I might have loved, you knew it, fleetingly!

CXIII. — SELF-COMMUNION

Be gentle, O my Sorrow; come now, settle down.
You pleaded for the Night: its shadows now appear.
A veil of darkness has descended on the town,
To some affording peace, to others care and fear.

While the vile multitude its recreation seeks
Beneath the cruel scourge of Pleasure's tyranny,
Garnering sore contrition in the servile feast,
My Sorrow, take my hand, and come away with me,

Far from them. See the bygone Years their vigil keep,
On heaven's balconies, in antiquated dress,
While simpering Regret emerges from the deep.

The dying Sun's last embers sink beneath an arch,
And, like an endless shroud trailing toward the East,
Hear, my beloved, hear Night's gentle onward march.

CXIV. — THE LABOURING SKELETON

I

In the old anatomic plates
Displayed along those dusty quays
With baubles and antiquities
And old tomes of uncertain date,

Where all the skill and all the art
Of the engraver's work appear
Which, though the subject is austere,
A certain Beauty still impart,

We see, to make the scene complete,
Like hideous automatons,
Skinless Corpses and Skeletons
Digging the earth with bony feet.

II

Out of this earth that you dig there,
Phantasmal peasants, spectral clones,
With all the effort of your bones
And of your muscles raw and bare,

What strange crop do you gather in
Like convicts from an ossuary,
And for what farmer's granary
Must you forever fill your bin?

Do you wish (emblems clear and pure
Of a too cruel destiny!)
To show that in eternity
Our promised sleep is still unsure;

That we're forsaken by the Void;
That even Death knows perfidy,
And that for all eternity
Alas! perhaps we'll be deployed

In some strange land, in searing heat,
To spend our days in heavy toil,
Digging the unforgiving soil
Beneath our naked, bleeding feet?

CXV. — EVENING TWILIGHT

Behold the charming evening, friend of villainy;
It comes like an accomplice, softly, stealthily;
The sky, like a great alcove, closes from the east,
And unforbearing man becomes a savage beast.

O cordial evening, so desired by those who say:
We have, without a doubt, done honest work today!
— It is the evening that brings comfort and relief
To those whose spirit is beset by pain and grief,
The conscientious sage who rests his weary head,
Or the stooped labourer relieved to find his bed.

Meanwhile repulsive demons waken from their sleep,
Reluctantly, like those who have to earn their keep,
Colliding into blinds and shutters in their flight.
The wind springs up to fan the street lamp's flickering light,
As Prostitution comes to life and spreads about,
A colony of ants letting its workers out,
In all directions carving out a secret track,
Like an invader planning a surprise attack;
It taints the city's heart with its clandestine plan,
Like a voracious worm that steals the food of Man.
We hear the sounds of sizzling kitchens here and there,
The clamour of theatres, orchestras ablare;
Cheap restaurants, where gamblers gather for their sport,
Begin to fill with harlots, swindlers and their sort,
And thieves, who never rest and know not charity,
Will soon begin their odious activity,
Stealthily forcing open strongboxes and doors
To eat for a few days and buy clothes for their whores.

In this dark hour, my soul, reflect on all this sin,
And close your ears to this cacophony of din.
This is the hour when sick men feel the greatest pain,
When dark Night grasps them by the throat, and they attain
Their final destined path toward the shared abyss;

Their sighs pervade the hospital. — No more the bliss
Of evenings spent at home, sharing a fragrant bowl
Of soup beside the fire, with a beloved soul.

But then, most of them are unable to recall
The comfort of the hearth and have not lived at all!

CXVI. — THE GAMING TABLE

On faded sofas, ladies of advancing years,
Pale, with come-hither eyes painted in lurid tones,
Flirtatious, simpering, impart from wizened ears
A jingle-jangle sound of gold and precious stones;

Visages without lips surrounding the green baize,
Lips that are drained of blood, and jaws of teeth bereft,
Convulsive fingers groping in a feverish daze
The empty pocket or the palpitating breast;

Beneath the grimy ceilings dingy lanterns glow,
And massive chandeliers project a lurid glare
Onto the sombre brows of famous men below,
Who come to squander all their sweat and lifeblood there;

Such was the lurid scene that in a dream one night
I saw before my visionary eyes unfold.
I saw myself there, in a corner out of sight,
My elbows on the table, silent, envious, cold,

Envious of the tenacious patience of those men,
And of those ageing whores the morbid gaiety,
All brazenly parading in that horrid den
The one his erstwhile honour, the other her lost beauty!

My heart was cowed with fear and shame for envying
Those wretched creatures, rushing to the great abyss,
Who, drunk on their own blood, would rather anything,
Pain, torment, even hell, to death and nothingness!

CXVII. — DANSE MACABRE

To Ernest Christophe

Proud, like a living being, of her noble stance,
With her bouquet of flowers, her handkerchief and gloves,
She has the easy manner and the nonchalance
Of a slender seductress flirting with her loves.

Was ever, at a ball, seen such a slender waist?
Her lavish drapery extravagantly flows
Upon her bony feet, which are daintily placed
In ornate slippers, decorated with a rose.

The frill that frames the contour of her clavicles,
Like a lascivious brooklet lapping on a rock,
Protects discreetly from unwanted ridicule
The charms she seeks to hide from those who like to mock.

Her hollow eyes are full of deep obscurity,
And her skull, set with flowers to such sublime effect,
Rocks gently to and fro on her frail vertebrae,
O charm of the unreal outlandishly bedecked!

There are some who will call you a caricature,
Lovers of flesh who are unable to admire
The nameless beauty of the human armature.
You are, great skeleton, all that I could desire!

Do you come, with your powerful grimace, to upset
The festival of Life? Or does some ancient fire,
Still burning in your living carcass, spur you yet
To credulously seek the Sabbath of Desire?

Do you hope that the violin's sweet melody,
Or the candle's bright flame, will banish your unrest,
And do you come to ask the floods of revelry
To quench the flames of hell that burn within your breast?

Immeasurable well of folly and of sin!
Untold distillery of ancient suffering!

Through the curved trellis of your ribs, I see therein
The insatiable viper ever wandering.

Indeed, to tell the truth, I fear your coquetry,
Despite its diligence, will not find just reward;
What mortal heart could understand your raillery?
For only to the strong does dread its charms accord!

Inducing vertigo, the chasms of your eyes
Conceal dark thoughts, and prudent dancers will revile,
With floods of bitter gall that in their souls arise,
The two-and-thirty teeth of your eternal smile.

But who's not held a skeleton in his embrace,
And who on sombre thoughts of tombs has never fed?
What matter fragrances, fine clothes of silk and lace?
Those who think they are handsome often scorn the dead.

O noseless bayadere, inexorable gouge,
Tell all these dancers who pretend to take offence:
"Proud dears, despite the art of powder and of rouge,
All of you smell of death! Skeletons filled with scents

Of musk, shrivelled Antinoüs, bald-pated beaux,
Varnished cadavers, old lovelaces with white hair,
This dance of death, this universal fandango
Leads you to places that you never knew were there!

And from the Seine's cold banks to Ganges' baking ground,
The herd of mortal men cavorts, oblivious
To the approach of the angelic trumpet sound
That threatens in the sky like a dark blunderbuss.

In all climes, under every sun, all-seeing Death
Admires your antics, risible Humanity,
And often, just like you, with perfume on her breath,
Mingles her irony with your insanity!"

CXVIII. — THE LOVE OF FALSEHOOD

When I see you, as on your languid way you go,
To the soft echo of a plaintive melody,
Suspending your demeanour, elegant and slow,
And showing in your gaze the depth of your ennui;

When I behold, lit by the gas-lamp's livid light,
Your pallid brow, embellished by a morbid trait,
Illumined, like a dawn, by lanterns of the night,
And your alluring eyes like those of a portrait,

I tell myself: how fair she is! how strangely fresh!
The towering memories that crown her from above
So regally; her heart, bruised like a ripened peach,
Is ready, like her body, for a knowing love.

Are you autumnal fruit, whose flavour is supreme?
A funeral urn awaiting tears in solemn hours,
A perfume that of far oases brings a dream,
Caressing pillow, or a basket full of flowers?

I know that there are eyes more wistful, melancholic,
That hold no mystery, in which no secret lies,
Like caskets without gems, or lockets without relics,
More empty, more profound than even you, O Skies!

But does it not suffice that you are an illusion
That renders gay a heart in flight from truth and duty?
What matter your indifference or your delusion?
Mask or adornment, hail! I venerate your beauty.

CXIX.

I never have forgot our little cottage there,
Close to the town, yet blessed with a most tranquil air;
A plaster Pomona and an old Aphrodite
Stood in a little copse, to hide their nudity,
And the late evening sun, whose slanting rays of gold
Behind the window pane were wondrous to behold,
Appeared to contemplate, with an inquiring eye,
Our silent evening meal from its home in the sky,
And, like a candle's glow, its mellow radiance cast
On the old tablecloth and our frugal repast.

CXX.

The servant with a heart of gold who sleeps alone,
Far from your jealous gaze, beneath a humble stone,
Should we not take her just a little bunch of flowers?
The dead, the wretched dead, endure such sombre hours,
And when the melancholy wind of autumn blows
Around the marble slab beneath which they repose,
The living must seem so ungrateful to the dead,
As they lie sleeping snug and cosy in their bed,
While they, the dead, gnawed by a sombre reverie,
Without a bedfellow to keep them company,
Frozen old skeletons upon whom worms have fed,
They feel the winter's snow that drips above their head,
The passing of the years, with neither family
Nor friend to tend their grave in the bleak cemetery.

If I saw her one evening, calmly sitting there
Beside the singing fire logs, in her rocking chair;
If, in the cheerless twilight of December's gloom,
I found her crouching in a corner of my room,
Forsaking the cold churchyard where she used to lie
To watch over her child with a maternal eye,
What would I find to say, after so many years,
To that devoted soul who sheds such loving tears?

CXXI. — THE OFFENDED MOON

O Moon that our forebears discreetly glorified,
From your blue confines where, serail in bright parade,
The stars attend you in resplendent cavalcade,
Old Cynthia, our lamp and our nocturnal guide,

Do you see lovers with their white enamelled teeth
That glow as they lie sleeping in their lavish bed?
The poet at his work beating his aching head?
Or vipers copulating on the arid heath?

Beneath your yellow veil, do you still steal away
Covertly, as of old, from dusk till break of day,
To kiss the faded charms of your Endymion?

— "I see thy mother, child of this poor century,
Bending toward her glass the weight of years now gone,
Artfully powdering the breast that suckled thee!"

CXXII. — MIST AND RAIN

O late autumnal days, winter and mud-soaked spring,
O dormant seasons, how I praise the joy you bring!
For you surround my heart and envelop my brain
In a vaporous shroud, a tomb of mist and rain.

Across this boundless plain where chill sou'westers course,
Where during endless nights the weathercock grows hoarse,
My spirit, more at ease with what the winter brings
Than with renascent springtime, opens wide its wings.

There's naught that's sweeter to a heart beset by doom,
So long acquainted with the hoarfrosts and the rimes,
O colourless seasons, pale monarchs of our climes,

Than the eternal aspect of your pallid gloom,
— Except perhaps, one moonless evening, head to head,
To put our woes to sleep on an intrepid bed.

CXXIII. — A PARISIAN DREAM

To Constantin Guys

I

Of that most awe-inspiring scene,
Such as mere mortals never see,
That lay before me in a dream,
The image still enraptures me.

Sleep is a miracle divine!
And, by a singular caprice,
I had excluded any sign
Of vegetation from the piece;

And, proud of my fine artistry,
I savoured in this rare tableau
The breathtaking monotony
Of metal, stone, and water-flow.

Babel of stairways and arcades
And endless palaces unrolled,
With limpid pools and great cascades
Falling on matte or burnished gold;

And even greater waterfalls,
Like crystal curtains hanging there,
Cascaded down metallic walls
As if suspended in the air.

The dormant pools, instead of trees
Were circumscribed by colonnades,
Where giant naiads took their ease,
Admiring their reflected gaze.

Lakes of blue water outward flowed
Between the rose and emerald quays,
Like an endless aquatic road,
To the earth's furthest boundaries;

Magical waves, embellished by
Exquisite gemstones that adorned
Enormous mirrors, dazzled by
The radiance of reflected forms.

Insouciant and taciturn,
Ganges flowed in the firmament,
Pouring the treasures from its urn
Into great gulfs of diamond.

Architect of my fantasy,
I made, out of a quiet rill,
To flow within an artery
An ocean I could tame at will;

And all the colours, even black,
Seemed iridescent, burnished bright;
The liquid gave its splendour back
In crystal rays of purest light.

No moon, no stars, nor any sign
Of sunlight to give luminance
To this prodigious scene of mine
That shone with its own radiance.

And on this wondrous vision here
There hovered (awful novelty!
All for the eye, naught for the ear!)
A silence of eternity.

II

I opened my bewildered eyes
And saw again the wretched hole
Wherein I dwelt, and felt arise
The pangs of anguish in my soul;

The melancholy clock struck noon
In accents brutal and perverse,
And from the sky a dreadful gloom
Pervaded the dull universe.

CXXIV. — MORNING TWILIGHT

Across the barracks yard the loud reveille came,
And the strong morning breeze disturbed the lantern's flame.

It was the hour when swarthy adolescent boys
Lie dreaming on their pillows of forbidden joys;
When, like a blood-shot eye that palpitates with dread,
The lantern on the daylight makes a patch of red;
And when the soul, weighed down by sombre disarray,
Mimics the combat of the lantern and the day.
Like weeping eyes upon whose tears the breezes play,
The trembling air pulsates with all that flees away,
Men tire of writing; women tire of lovers' play.

Chimneys began to smoke as night gave way to day.
Women of pleasure, eyelids painted vulgarly,
Were sleeping, open-mouthed, in stupid reverie,
While others, destitute, their bosoms cold and blue,
Breathed on the dying embers, and on their fingers too.
It was the hour when, due to cold and penury,
Women in childbirth are more prone to agony;
And like a sob that's choked by frothy blood and gall,
A distant rooster pierced the dank air with its call;
A sea of fog enveloped windows, doors and walls,
And those who agonised inside the hospitals
Uttered the final rattle of their wretched lives.
The weary debauchees returned home to their wives.

Aurora, shivering in robe of rose and green,
Slowly advanced along the still deserted Seine,
And sombre Paris rubbed his eyes as day began,
And gathered up his tools, industrious old man.

EPILOGUE

With heart content I climbed up to the citadel,
Whence I surveyed the town in all its amplitude,
Hospital, brothel, jail, abyss, perdition, hell,

Where bloom the evil flowers of human turpitude.
O Satan, you know well, as master of my pain,
That I did not go there to shed an idle tear,

But like an aging rake with his old chatelaine,
I wanted to grow drunk on that great concubine,
Whose infamous allurements give me youth again.

And whether in the sheets of morning you recline
In heavy slumber still, or strut flamboyantly
In evening's braided veil, enlaced with golden twine,

I love you, capital of vice and infamy!
Your villains and your whores afford felicities
Unknown to any brute or vulgar philistine.

WINE

CXXV. — THE SOUL OF WINE

One night the soul of wine was singing in the flasks:
"O Man, I send to you, in your most wretched state,
From my glass prison, sealed by the vermilion wax,
A poem full of light and brotherly estate!

I know how much devotion, how much sweat and toil,
Upon the burning hill, beneath a leaden sun,
Is needed to engender in me life and soul;
But I am not ungrateful, when all's said and done,

For I am filled with joy when gladly I succumb
Upon the eager throat of one consumed by toil,
Whose warm oesophagus provides a pleasant tomb
Where I am more content than in the cellar's chill.

Do you not hear the hope that beats within my heart?
The sound of merriment in Sunday's happy song?
Sleeves rolled and glasses raised you'll celebrate my art
And glorify my name in verses loud and long;

I shall inspire delight in your dear lady's eyes,
Restore unto your son his colour and aplomb,
And that frail athlete of this life will surely prize
This oil that firms the flesh and makes the muscles strong.

In you I shall descend, ambrosia of the earth,
A precious seed that's sown by the eternal sower,
So that out of our love a poem shall have birth,
Ascending heavenward to God like a rare flower!"

CXXVI. — THE RAG-PICKERS' WINE

Often, beneath a street-lamp's flickering red flame,
As the night wind springs up, disturbing the glass frame,
In the old quarter's muddy, labyrinthine maze
Where in a seething ferment swarms the human race,

One comes upon a ragman, nodding busily,
Stumbling and bumping into pillars, carelessly,
And, paying no attention to disloyal sneaks,
He pours his heart out in the plans of which he speaks.

He swears a solemn oath, proclaiming laws sublime,
Roundly denounces crooks, supports victims of crime,
And underneath the sky's suspended canopy
Grows drunk on his own virtue and integrity.

Yes, these men, burdened by the chores of daily life,
Worn out by age and tormented by toil and strife,
Weighed down by all their woes, beset by fear and doubt,
Crushed by the piles of dross that Paris vomits out,

Return, redolent with the odour of the cask,
With their comrades-in-arms, pale from their daily task,
Whose whiskers droop like faded pennants as they march.
The banderols, the flowers and a triumphal arch

Rise up before their eyes, in solemn majesty!
And in the deafening and luminous orgy
Of trumpets, drums and cries, and sunlight from above,
They bring a taste of glory to a people drunk with love!

And so it is that wine, like Pactolus of old,
Bathes frivolous Mankind in dazzling streams of gold,
And in men's throats of noble deeds is wont to sing,
And by dint of its prowess reigns just like a king.

To drown their bitter thoughts and calm antipathy
In all those blighted souls who die in misery,
God, in remorse, invented sleep for everyone;
And then Man added Wine, sacred child of the Sun!

CXXVII. — THE MURDERER'S WINE

My wife is dead, and I am free!
Now I'll be plastered all the time.
When I came home without a dime,
Her wailing used to torture me.

I am as happy as a king;
The air is pure, the sky is blue…
Just like that summer when I knew
That a romance was blossoming!

This awful thirst that grows apace
Would need, to quench it, truth be told,
As much wine as her tomb could hold;
— And that's a pretty roomy place:

I threw her body down a well,
I even pushed on top of it
As many stones as I could fit.
— Will I forget her? Time will tell!

By virtue of our solemn oath
That nothing ever can defile,
And so that we might reconcile
Ourselves, as when we pledged our troth,

I asked to meet her once again,
One night in a secluded place.
She came — mad creature! (grant her grace!).
We are all more or less insane!

She was still such a pretty wife,
Though rather tired and worn! And I
Loved her too much! And that is why
I said to her: Depart this life!

No-one can understand my mind.
Did any sot, addled by drink,
In his most morbid fancy think
To make a winding-sheet of wine?

That unshakable philistine,
Impervious as a steel machine,
Even in his most ardent dream,
Love's raptures never could divine,

With its enchantments and its pains,
Its winding trail of doubts and fears,
Its poisoned chalices, its tears,
Its sounds of rattling bones and chains.

— So here I am, free and alone!
Tonight I'll be blind drunk, of course;
And then, without fear or remorse,
I shall lie down on the cold stone,

And there I'll sleep, out like a light!
The heavy wheels of a huge truck,
Loaded with earth and stones and muck,
Careering down the highway, might

As well shatter my guilty head
Or slice my body clean in two,
I've had enough of all of you,
God, Satan and the Holy Bread!

CXXVIII. — THE LONELY MAN'S WINE

A handsome courtesan's intoxicating gaze
That glides toward us like the pale transparent beam
The undulating moon sends to the trembling stream,
Where carelessly she bathes the beauty of her rays;

The final bag of florins in a gambler's hand,
Or a wanton embrace from slender Annaliese;
The gentle yet unnerving sounds of melodies,
Like cries of human sorrow from some distant land;

None of these things, O bottle wide and deep, is worth
The penetrating balm that your abundant girth
Reserves for the devoted poet's thirsting heart;

You give him youth and hope, those enemies of doubt,
— And pride, that priceless treasure of the down-and-out,
That gives us grandeur and, like gods, sets us apart!

CXXIX. — THE LOVERS' WINE

How splendid is the world today!
Without bit or spur, lets away
Upon our mounts of heady wine
To heavens magic and divine!

Like two angels tormented by
An ardent flame that will not die,
In the bright morning's crystal blue
Let us the far mirage pursue.

Riding and rocking languidly
On an all-knowing, swirling tide,
In a parallel ecstasy,

My sister, floating side by side,
We'll follow these exotic streams
To the nirvana of my dreams!

FLOWERS OF EVIL

CXXX. — THE SUNSET OF ROMANTICISM

How beautiful and fresh the rising sun's soft gleam,
Embracing the new day with greetings from above!
— O happy is the man who can with thoughts of love
Salute its going down, more glorious than a dream!

I do recall that I have seen, at close of day,
Spring, furrow, flower, swooning like a beating heart
Beneath its gaze… — 'Tis late, come quickly, let's depart
To the horizon, to catch one last slanting ray!

But I pursue that sinking Deity in vain;
Inexorable Night lays claim to her domain,
Dark, humid, sinister and filled with trembling fear;

In the vast darkness floats an odour of the tomb,
And my uncertain footsteps trample in the gloom
Cold snails and unseen toads beside a muddy mere.

CXXXI. — DESTRUCTION

Forever at my side, the Devil does not rest;
He hovers over me with his mysterious fire;
I breathe him in and feel him burning in my breast,
Pervading me with endless, culpable desire.

Sometimes, knowing my love of Art, he takes the shape
Of an alluring woman, proud, promiscuous,
And under specious pretexts that I can't escape,
Acquaints my eager lips with philtres infamous.

He leads me thus, far from the watchful eye of God,
Panting, and broken with fatigue, on paths untrod,
Amid the plains of Ennui, fearful and alone,

And casts before my horrified, bewildered eyes
Filthy apparel, gaping wounds of blood and bone,
And all of foul Destruction's hideous supplies!

CXXXII. — A MARTYR

Drawing by an unknown Master

Amid the perfume flasks, the fabrics of lamé,
The furnishings of wealth untold,
The marbles, paintings, and the fine-scented array
Of dresses, fold on sumptuous fold,

In a room where the air is dank and vaporous,
Where fatal omens multiply,
Where dying bouquets in their glass sarcophagus
Exhale their last expiring sigh,

A headless corpse pours out, in a cascade that bursts
Onto the covers of the bed,
A tide of blood on which the fabric slakes its thirst,
A living stream of vibrant red.

Like those pale visions that entrap our curious stare,
Visions born of obscurity,
The head, with its thick mass of dark, luxuriant hair
And its expensive jewellery,

Upon a small commode, like a ranunculus,
Is resting. From unseeing eyes
A vague, bewildered look, both pale and tenebrous,
Expresses horror and surprise.

The naked torso, on the bed, lies motionless,
Displaying, by a lantern lit,
The secret splendour and the fatal comeliness
That nature had bestowed on it;

A rose-hued stocking, flecked with gold, adorns the thigh,
Like a macabre souvenir;
The garter, glistening like a secretive eye,
Emits a diamantine leer.

The singular aspect of all this solitude
And the portrait that hangs above,
With its strange eyes and its alluring attitude,
Tokens of a tenebrous love,

Reveal clandestine joys and esoteric rites,
Demonic lecheries untold,
Of which malignant angels savoured the delights,
Secreted in the curtains' folds;

And yet, to judge by the seductive shapeliness
Of the exquisite shoulder's rake,
The slightly pointed hips, the waistline's slenderness,
Suggestive of a writhing snake,

She is still young! — Did her exasperated soul,
Her senses, gnawed by deep ennui,
Give way to wandering desires, losing control
In frenzies of debauchery?

That vengeful man whose lust, living, you could not sate
Despite much love, nor quench his fire,
Did he upon your yielding body consummate
The magnitude of his desire?

Reply, impure cadaver! By your abundant hair
Uplifting you with fevered fist,
Tell me, macabre head, did he, holding you there,
Plant on your teeth his farewell kiss?

— Far from the sneering world, the saturnalian crowd,
The curious inquisitor,
Sleep, bizarre creature, sleep in peace beneath the shroud
Of your mysterious sepulchre;

Your spouse will roam the world, and your immortal wraith
Will watch his every sleeping breath;
No doubt, as you do, he will likewise keep the faith,
And remain constant until death.

CXXXIII. — LESBOS

Mother of Latin games and Greek voluptuousness,
Lesbos, where long caresses bring such sweet delights,
Some full of ardent passion, some full of tenderness,
To glorious summer days and sultry wanton nights.
Mother of Latin games and Greek voluptuousness,

Lesbos, where love's caresses flow like cataracts,
Cascading fearlessly into the deep abyss,
Rebounding, sobbing, laughing, making secret pacts,
Delighting in the storms engendered by each kiss.
Lesbos, where love's caresses flow like cataracts!

Lesbos, where every Phryne has her concubine,
Where never did a sigh remain without echo,
You equal starlit Paphos in your grace divine,
And Venus might be justly envious of Sappho!
Lesbos, where every Phryne has her concubine,

Lesbos, exotic land of sultry, languid nights,
Where, in their looking-glass, O sterile wantonness!
Young girls with hollow eyes, in love with their delights,
Bestow upon their nubile charms a soft caress;
Lesbos, exotic land of sultry, languid nights,

Let old austere Plato knit his brow in a frown;
Your pardon can be found in kisses and caresses,
Queen of this gentle empire, fair land of great renown,
And in refinements that know nothing of excesses.
Let old austere Plato knit his brow in a frown.

Your pardon can be found in the eternal pain
Suffered by hearts in which too much ambition lies,
Lured, by a radiant smile, from their secure domain,
That beckons from the confines of more distant skies!
Your pardon can be found in the eternal pain!

Which of the Gods, O Lesbos, will dare to be your judge,
Condemning your pale brow, that has toiled ceaselessly,
Before his golden scales have weighed the heavy flood
Of tears that from your streams have flowed into the sea?
Which of the Gods, Lesbos, will dare to be your judge?

What care we for the laws of what's just and unjust?
Maidens of whose renown these islands proudly tell,
Your faith, as any faith, is noble and august,
And love can laugh at Heaven as it can laugh at Hell!
What care we for the laws of what's just or unjust?

For Lesbos chose me from all poets on the earth
To praise the flowering virgins that this isle reveres,
For I have known the mystery, almost from birth,
Of their unbridled laughter and their sombre tears;
For Lesbos chose me from all poets on the earth.

And since then I keep watch from the Leucadian height,
Like a lone sentry with a sure and piercing gaze,
For frigates, brigs and tartanes coming into sight,
Whose distant silhouettes appear to flutter in the haze.
And since then I keep watch from the Leucadian height

To divine if the sea is good and bountiful,
If in the sobbing of its waves it is kind-hearted,
And will return to Lesbos, who is merciful,
The venerated corpse of Sappho, who departed
To divine if the sea is good and bountiful!

Of virile Sappho, paramour and poetess,
More beautiful than Venus in her pale despondency!
— The azure eyes are vanquished by the dolefulness
Of the dark circles that betray the misery
Of virile Sappho, paramour and poetess!

More beautiful than Venus, holding sway above the world
And pouring forth the wealth of her serenity,
With the effulgence of her youthful locks unfurled,
On the old Ocean, proud of his child's majesty;
More beautiful than Venus, holding sway above the world!

Of Sappho who succumbed to blasphemy that day,
When, scornful of her cult, her faith, her loyalty,
She wantonly allowed her body to fall prey
To a proud brute who punished the impiety
Of her who did succumb to blasphemy that day.

And it is since that day that Lesbos must lament;
Though honoured by the world, she must for evermore
Endure each night the cries of anguish and torment
That rise toward the sky from her deserted shore!
And it is since that day that Lesbos must lament!

CXXXIV. — DAMNED WOMEN I

Like contemplative beasts recumbent on the sands,
They scan the skyline of the ocean with their eyes,
And feet caressing feet, and hands entwined in hands,
They temper bitter thoughts with gentle languid sighs.

Some, whose hearts are engaged in long communion,
Deep in secluded groves where babbling brooklets flow,
Inscribing childlike words of love and union
Upon the virgin bark where verdant saplings grow;

Others, like nuns, walk slowly, gravely and in fear
Across the rocky paths beneath the mountain crests,
Where once Saint Anthony in visions saw appear,
To tempt him, an array of naked rose-hued breasts;

Some there are who, lit by a resin lamp's dull flame,
Deep in the silent hollow of some pagan place,
To calm their wretched fevers loudly call your name,
O Bacchus, sleep-inducing healer of malaise!

And others, with a liking for monastic dress,
Who, with a whip concealed in their accoutrement,
Mingle, in sombre woods and nights of loneliness,
The froth of pleasure with the tears of their torment.

O virgins, demons, monsters, martyrs, debauchees,
Great spirits who are scornful of reality,
Seeking infinity, sirens and devotees,
Now uttering loud cries, now weeping bitterly,

Poor sisters, whom my soul has followed in your hell,
I love you and I pity you in equal parts,
For all your dark despair, your thirsts life cannot quell,
And those great urns of love that fill your bounteous hearts!

CXXXV. — DAMNED WOMEN II (Delphine and Hippolyta)

In the pale, languid glow of lamps in deep recesses,
On lavish cushions that were redolent with scents,
Hippolyta lay dreaming of the bold caresses
That drew aside the veil of her young innocence.

She sought, her troubled gaze blurred by the storm, the skies
Of her virginity, already far away,
As might a voyager who vainly turns his eyes
Toward the blue horizons passed earlier in the day.

The idle tears that filled her dull eyes, once so bright,
The broken look, the stupor, the weary wantonness,
Her arms, like useless weapons cast aside in flight,
All serving to adorn her fragile comeliness.

Languidly, at her feet, Delphine contented lay,
Ardently watching her, eyes blazing with delight,
Like a strong, savage beast that gazes on its prey,
On which its teeth have left the imprint of its bite.

Strong beauty proudly kneeling at frail beauty's feet,
Savouring the bouquet, voluptuous and lewd,
Of her triumphant wine, and in her vain conceit
Soliciting a token of sweet gratitude.

Expectantly she sought in her pale victim's eye
The silent canticle that purest pleasure sings,
And the infinite gratitude that, like a sigh,
Escapes in subtle glances from mysterious springs.

— "Hippolyta, dear heart, what say you of these things?
Do you now understand you must not sacrifice
The sacred holocaust of your first flowerings
To harsh caresses that exact a heavy price?

My kisses are as gentle as the mayfly's wings
That silently caress the surface of the lake,
While those of a male lover wreak destructive things,
Like the deep grooves that chariots and ploughshares make.

They'll trample over you, like a lumbering team
Of horses and of oxen, their hooves with iron shod...
Hippolyta, my sister! My sweet enduring dream,
My spirit and my soul, my wondrous gift from God,

Turn unto me your eyes of starlight and azure!
For one beguiling glance, divine balm, radiant beam,
I shall unveil a store of pleasures more obscure,
And lull you gently in a never-ending dream!"

Then said Hippolyta, raising her youthful head:
— "It's not ingratitude or remorse that I feel,
My Delphine, yet I suffer and am filled with dread
After this dark and terrible nocturnal meal.

I feel a heavy torment hanging over me
And dark battalions of vague demonic shapes
Leading me down strange pathways of uncertainty,
Hemmed in by horizons from which there's no escape.

Have we therefore engaged in an illicit pleasure?
Tell me, why do I feel such sorrow and such fear?
I tremble when I hear you say to me: 'My treasure!'
And yet my lips are drawn to yours when you are near.

Do not behold me thus, my dearest sister whom
I shall forever hold in deepest adoration,
Even were you to be a snare set for my doom
And the beginning of my eternal damnation!"

Delphine arose and proudly shook her tragic mane,
And wildly seeking what the tripod might foretell,
With fatal eye, responded in despotic vein:
— "Who in love's presence dares to speak the name of hell?

May he be ever cursed who fostered useless dreams,
Who was the first to try, in his stupidity,
To fashion sterile edicts and misguided schemes
That mingle things erotic with integrity!

He who would merge into a mystical accord
The sun's heat with the shade, the daytime with the night,
Will never warm himself nor garner a reward
Beneath this radiant sun of amorous delight!

Go, if you wish, and seek a stupid paramour;
Offer your virgin heart to his cruel caress;
And, filled with dire remorse, repentance and dolour,
You will bring back to me your violated breasts...

A woman here on earth can only serve one master!"
But the sweet child, by anxious torment torn apart,
Cried suddenly: — "I feel, opening ever faster,
A yawning chasm; and that chasm is my heart!

Neither the depths of hell, nor the volcano's rage
Will ever satisfy this groaning monster's ire!
And nothing can the Fury's dreadful thirst assuage,
Who, flaming torch in hand, consumes its blood with fire.

Let our drawn curtains set us from the world apart,
And may our lassitude bring us eternal rest!
I want to sleep forever in your beating heart,
And feel the coolness of the tomb upon your breast!"

— Descend, descend, pitiful victims, it is time
To fathom the abyss of hell's eternal fire!
Plunge into its vast depths where every human crime,
Whipped by a wind too fierce even for heaven's ire,

Bubbles and effervesces in a storm-like rage.
Mad shadows, your desires will not be compromised;
Never will you be able your passions to assuage,
And by your very pleasures you will be chastised.

No ray of light can penetrate your dismal lair,
Only feverish miasma passing through small vents,
Dimly illumining the dark and fetid air,
And covering your bodies with their lurid scents.

The harsh sterility of your lasciviousness
Quickens your raging thirst and vitrifies your skin,
And the unbridled wind of your licentiousness
Causes your flesh to flap in penance for its sin.

In exile from this world, you must your path pursue
Through wild and barren lands, wandering aimlessly,
Fleeing the infinite that still resides in you,
Poor disconnected souls, to find your destiny!

CXXXVI. — THE MONSTER
or The Paranymph of a Macabre Nymph

I

'Tis certain, my dear, you are not
What Veuillot calls a tenderling.
Bubbling in your old cooking-pot
Are gambling, sex and merrying!
So, my old darling, you are not

So fresh these days. However, dear,
Your antics, that leave me bemused,
Lend you that most lustrous veneer
Of things that are very well-used
But which still have their charm, my dear.

I do not find that it grows stale,
That green your forty summers bring;
Your autumn fruits to me unveil
More pleasures than the flowers of spring
No! you are never dull nor stale.

Your fine physique can still entice
With charms that I cannot disown;
I find a strange exotic spice
In the curve of your collar bone;
Your fine physique can still entice!

To hell with those pathetic fools,
Who thrive on melon and courgette!
I much prefer your clavicles
To those of Solomon the Great;
I pity those pathetic fools!

Like a blue helmet is the hair
That frames your warrior-like face
(Where thoughts and blushes are so rare),
Then sweeps back to its hiding-place.
Like a blue helmet is your hair!

As black as peat moss are your eyes,
Wherein a beacon shimmers bright
And with your farded cheeks allies,
Emitting an infernal light!
As black as peat moss are your eyes.

With wantonness and pure disdain
Your bitter lips provoke our lust;
They are like Eden born again,
Inspiring passion and disgust.
What wantonness! And what disdain!

Your legs, robust and sinewy,
Could climb to a volcano's top,
And despite snow and penury,
Dance a lively cancan nonstop.
Your legs are strong and sinewy;

Your burning skin lacks tenderness,
Like an old constable's veneers;
It's never felt sudor's caress
Just as your eyes have not known tears.
(And yet there is some tenderness!)

II

You fool, you're headed straight for hell!
I'd willingly go with you too,
If this formidable pell-mell
Did not cause me to pause anew.
So off you go, alone, to hell!

My loins and lungs do not afford
Me strength to praise the hallowed name,
With due respect, of that great Lord.
"Alas! It really is a shame!"
My loins and lungs say in accord.

Oh! most sincerely do I suffer
Not to be going to the mass,
To see, when he is farting sulphur,
How you might kiss his stinking ass!
Oh! most sincerely do I suffer!

I am most devilishly aggrieved
Not to become your guiding light,
And have to ask you for your leave,
Infernal torch! Judge how I might
Feel more than devilishly aggrieved;

Since I have loved you for so long,
It's logical, it seems to me,
To seek the cream of Evil's wrong
And worship pure monstrosity,
Old monster, yes! I've loved you long!

CXXXVII. — A PAGAN'S PRAYER

Ah! do not damp thy ardent coals;
Warm my cold heart, I beg of thee,
Indulgence, tormentor of souls!
Diva! Supplicem exaudi!

Goddess, who in the clear air dwell,
Burn also in our caverns dim!
All brooding from this soul dispel,
That offers thee this brazen hymn.

Joy, be my queen, that's all I ask!
Pleasure, put on a siren's mask
Of velvet and soft flesh composed,

Or else pour me the deep repose
Of an amorphous, mystic wine,
Elastic phantom, Joy divine!

CXXXVIII. — THE METAMORPHOSES OF THE VAMPIRE

The woman, meanwhile, from alluring strawberry lips,
Like a snake on hot coals writhing her waist and hips,
Pressing her breasts into the metal of her busk,
Let flow these words infused with a bouquet of musk:
— "Behold, my lips are moist, and I have learned the art
Of swooning to the joys seduction can impart.
I dry everyone's tears on my triumphant breasts,
And I make old men laugh, as children laugh at jests.
Divested of attire, my naked form would vie
With the sun and the moon, and the stars and the sky!
I am, my learned friend, so versed in wanton charms,
That when I hold a mortal in my fearsome arms,
Or when I offer up to avid bites my bust,
Timid yet libertine, both fragile and robust,
Upon these mattresses, that swoon in ecstasy,
Debilitated angels would damn themselves for me!"

But when she had sucked all the marrow out of me,
And when again I turned toward her languidly
To render her a loving kiss, I could see just
A viscous, oozing wineskin, full of fetid pus!
I closed my eyes in horror at the ghastly sight,
And when I opened them again, in the harsh light,
Instead of a voluptuous woman by my side,
Whose vampire lust I thought my blood had satisfied,
There trembled in confusion a skeleton's remains,
From which came a loud rattle, like a weathervane
Or a shop sign suspended from an iron spike,
Buffeted by the wind on a wild winter's night.

CXXXIX. — THE TWO GOOD SISTERS

Debauchery and Death are two endearing twins,
Replete with the delights and pleasures of this earth,
Whose rag-clad virgin loins, unsullied by their sins,
Forever labouring, have never given birth.

To the sinister poet, foe of families,
Favoured by the abyss, sycophant on low pay,
Both tomb and bawdy house show in their sanctuaries
A bed in which remorse and penance never lay.

The alcove and the bier, both rich in blasphemy,
Offer us each in turn, like sisters good and true,
Sweet lusts and dreadful pleasures to enchant anew.

When will you bury me, corrupt Debauchery?
O Death, who rival her allure, when will it be
That you graft your black cypress on her myrtle tree?

CXL. — THE REBEL

An Angel, eagle-like, swoops furious from the sky,
Seizes the rascal's hair abruptly in his fist,
And, shaking him, says: "With my rule you shall comply!
(For I am your good Angel, do you hear?) I insist!

Know that you must show love, and do not pull a face!
To paupers, rogues and those cursed by insanity,
So that for Jesus, when he passes, you can place
Before him your triumphal cloak of charity.

For such is Love! Before your heart becomes blasé,
Rekindle your devotion to God's glorious way;
That is the lasting Joy, and the devout man's lot!"

The Angel then, whose wrath is equal to his love,
Rains down upon the sinner harsh blows from above;
But the accursèd one still answers: "I will not!"

CXLI. — THE FOUNTAIN OF BLOOD

Sometimes it seems to me my blood is running free,
Bubbling as from a fountain, sobbing rhythmically.
I hear it flowing like a steady stream of rain,
But though I seek the wound, I always seek in vain.

Across the city streets, as in a battle zone,
It goes, making an island of each paving stone,
Quenching the thirst of every living creature there,
And colouring in crimson nature everywhere.

I've often asked for succour from beguiling wine
To dull the pain I feel, if only for a night!
But wine augments the hearing and enhances sight!

I've sought in carnal love oblivion divine;
But love for me is but a painful bed of thorns
Designed to slake the thirst of those bloodthirsty whores!

CXLII. — ALLEGORY

Picture a woman whose allurements are divine,
Her silken tresses trailing in her scarlet wine.
The claws of love, the poisons of those dens of sin,
Slide over and are blunted on her granite skin.
She treats Death with disdain and mocks Debauchery,
Those monsters whose strong hands are working constantly
At their destructive games, yet have shown fealty
To her exquisite body's untamed majesty.
A goddess when she walks, a sultana at leisure,
She shows unyielding faith in her pursuit of pleasure;
Her eyes, her ample breasts, and her wide-open arms
Invite the human race to celebrate her charms.
She thinks, indeed she knows, that she cannot give birth
And yet she is so vital to this complex earth;
She knows that woman's beauty is a gift sublime
That warrants absolution from all heinous crime.
She knows nothing of Hell, nor yet of Purgatory,
And when her time is come to face eternity,
She'll look Death in the face, and she'll accept her fate,
Just like a new-born child, — without remorse or hate.

CXLIII. — THE BEATRICE

As through a barren land I wandered aimlessly,
Berating nature and complaining bitterly,
Sharpening slowly on the whetstone of my heart
The knife with which my thoughts were tearing me apart,
I saw, in the full noon, descending on my head,
A huge macabre cloud that filled my soul with dread,
For therein I beheld a veritable horde
Of vicious dwarf-like demons, nodding in accord.
Sullenly they began to look me up and down,
And, just as passers-by might stop to watch a clown,
I heard them sniggering and talking quietly,
Exchanging gestures as their eyes examined me:

— "Let's take a while to contemplate this travesty
Who Hamlet's tragic posture seeks to parody,
With indecisive look and long, dishevelled hair.
Is it not pitiful to see the anxious stare
Of this penniless hack trying to play a part?
For he's convinced that he is practised in his art,
Seeking to entertain, with his dull tales of woe,
The eagles, crickets, flowers, even the streams that flow,
And even we, the authors of these old conceits,
Must hear the long tirades he shouts about the streets!"

I could (being the lord and master of my pride
That soars above the peaks and clouds) have turned aside
Serenely from those demons' insults, and ignored
Their jibes, had I not seen, among that loathsome horde,
O crime that did not even cause the sun to move!
The queen of my desire, my one and only love,
Laughing aloud with them and mocking my distress,
And even sharing with them an obscene caress.

CXLIV. — A VOYAGE TO CYTHERA

My spirit, like a bird, was winging joyfully,
Hovering free about the rigging, soaring high;
Our ship sailed peacefully beneath a cloudless sky,
An angel spellbound by the sun's resplendency.

What is this gloomy isle, this sombre port of call?
— It's Cythera, we're told, a land famous in song,
Banal utopia for which old roués long.
But look, it's just a dismal country after all.

— Island of tender secrets and pageants of the heart!
The proud spirit of Venus hovers fragrantly
Above your fabled seas, as in antiquity,
Upon enchanted souls love's languor to impart.

Fair isle of myrtles green and flowers that disclose
Their charms to every nation's venerating eyes,
Where of adoring hearts the ever-loving sighs
Imbue with incense gardens of sweet-scented rose

Or mingle sweetly with a dove's eternal moan!
— Cythera had become a landscape bleak and bare,
A rock-strewn desert where shrill cries pervade the air.
However, I discerned something that stood alone!

It was no ancient temple shaded by tall trees,
Where a young priestess, lover of exotic flowers,
Obsessed by secret dreams, might while away the hours,
Her silken robe half open to the passing breeze;

For when we were as close to shore as we could get,
Our silver sails dispersing ravens in their flight,
We saw a three-armed gibbet standing there, upright
Against the azure sky, in sombre silhouette.

Ferocious birds were perched upon their carrion prey,
A rotting corpse that must have hung there for a week,
Each planting the sharp point of its repulsive beak
Into each bloody corner of that foul decay;

The eyes were just two holes, and from the open loin
The intestines spilled out and fell onto the thighs,
And his torturers had, O hideous surprise!
Ripped out the very manhood from his gaping groin.

Beneath the feet, a herd of jealous quadrupeds
Circled impatiently, sniffing the putrid air;
And a much larger beast, prowling amongst them there,
Seemed like an executioner among his aides.

Native of Cythera, child of its bounteous womb,
You suffered silently and paid an awful price
In expiation for your infamy and vice,
And all the sins that have deprived you of a tomb.

Ridiculous hanged man, I share all of your pain!
And, seeing your limbs hanging there, I must confess
I felt the nausea ascending in my breast,
The gall of former sorrows rising once again;

Poor devil, you stirred in me memories afresh;
I felt each pecking beak and every gnashing tooth
Of those rapacious crows and panthers of my youth,
Who once took such delight in savouring my flesh.

— The sky was azure blue, and calm suffused the sea;
For me all had become a bloodstained, sombre cloud,
Alas! and as if wrapped in a funereal shroud,
My heart was buried deep inside this allegory.

O Venus, I found nothing on your island! Just
A token gibbet from which hung my effigy...
— O Lord! give me the strength and the tenacity
To view my body and my soul without disgust!

CXLV. — LOVE AND THE SKULL

Old Tailpiece

Love is seated on the skull
Of Humanity;
Thus enthroned this heathen, full
Of effrontery,

Blows round bubbles that unfurl
And ascend apace,
As if seeking other worlds
In the depths of space.

This translucent fragile sphere
Takes its rapid flight,
Bursts, and spits its contents clear
Out into the night.

When each bubble bursts, the skull
Trembles, and entreats:
— "This mad game is pitiful,
When is it to cease?

For what your foul bubbles rain
Down in copious flood,
Vile assassin, is my brain,
My flesh and my blood!"

REVOLT

CXLVI. — SAINT PETER'S DENIAL

What then does God do with this flood of blasphemies
That rises daily to his Seraphim divine?
Like any tyrant who has gorged on meat and wine,
He falls asleep, lulled by our vile profanities.

The sobs of martyrs and the cries of tortured men
Are doubtless an intoxicating symphony
Because, though for their sins they have paid heavily,
The heavens have by no means had their fill of them!

— Jesus, think of the Garden of Gethsemane!
When you knelt down to pray, in all simplicity,
To him who in his heaven mocked your misery
When into your live flesh the nails sank painfully;

When you heard men deriding your divinity,
Blackguards and ruffians who wished to see you dead,
And when you felt the thorns sink deep into your head,
In which there dwelt the whole of our Humanity;

When the weight of your broken body, once so proud,
Stretched your extended arms, and when your sweat and blood
Flowed from your livid brow in an incessant flood,
When you were raised in martyrdom before the crowd,

Did you dream of those glorious days and wondrous hours
When you came to fulfil the covenant of God,
When, seated on an ass, in majesty you trod
The streets bestrewn with palms and garlanded with flowers,

When, buoyed by faith and hope, devoid of doubt or fear,
You castigated money-lenders with such force,
In other words, when you were master? Did remorse
Not pierce your side far deeper than the soldier's spear?

— For my part, I shall leave this world well satisfied,
This world where dream and action dwell in disaccord;
Let me live by the sword and perish by the sword!
Saint Peter denied Jesus... he was justified!

CXLVII. — ABEL AND CAIN

I

Tribe of Abel, eat, drink and sleep;
God smiles on you indulgently.

Tribe of Cain, slither and creep
Through the mire; die miserably.

Tribe of Abel, your sacrifice
Is pleasing to the Seraphim!

Tribe of Cain, when will the price
That you must pay satisfy Him?

Tribe of Abel, your flocks thrive
And your healthy crops abound;

Tribe of Cain, to stay alive
You eat the scraps that you have found.

Tribe of Abel, take your ease
At the patriarchal fire;

Tribe of Cain, tremble and freeze
Like a jackal in the mire!

Tribe of Abel, love, increase!
Your gold brings forth new progeny.

Tribe of Cain, take heed and cease
Your appetite for cruelty.

Abel's tribe, you feed and grow
Like insects boring endlessly!

Tribe of Cain, your people go
In fear and insecurity.

II

Tribe of Abel, your remains
Will fertilise the steaming soil!

Tribe of Cain, it still remains
For you to profit from your toil;

Tribe of Abel, to your shame
The plough is vanquished by the sword!

Tribe of Cain, now stake your claim
To heaven, and cast out the Lord!

CXLVIII. — THE LITANIES OF SATAN

O fairest of all Angels, wise in all your ways,
Spirit betrayed by destiny, deprived of praise,

O Satan, pity me in my long misery!

O Prince of exile who from men have suffered wrong
And who, vanquished, always stand up again more strong,

O Satan, pity me in my long misery!

O great all-knowing king of subterranean things,
Familiar healer of all human sufferings,

O Satan, pity me in my long misery!

You who give lepers and all those whom men despise,
Through your eternal love, a taste of Paradise,

O Satan, pity me in my long misery!

You who, even from Death, your old and trusted mate,
Knew how to fashion Hope, - that charming opiate!

O Satan, pity me in my long misery!

You who lend the doomed man a bearing calm and proud
Upon the scaffold, bringing shame upon the crowd,

O Satan, pity me in my long misery!

You who know in what corners of this envious earth
A jealous God secreted gemstones of great worth,

O Satan, pity me in my long misery!

You whose clear eye can see the arsenals and stores
Where lie, in slumber deep, great tribes of precious ores,

O Satan, pity me in my long misery!

You whose broad hand conceals the fatal precipice
From the sleep-walker lost atop an edifice,

O Satan, pity me in my long misery!

You who know how to render supple ageing bones
Of drunks trampled by horses on the cobblestones,

O Satan, pity me in my long misery!

You who, to comfort frail and suffering mankind,
Taught us how sulphur and saltpetre are combined,

O Satan, pity me in my long misery!

You who inscribe your mark, O comrade full of guile,
On the brow of a Croesus, pitiless and vile,

O Satan, pity me in my long misery!

You who, upon the eyes and hearts of kindly whores,
Bestowed a love of ragged clothes and bleeding sores,

O Satan, pity me in my long misery!

Staff of the exiled, guiding lamp of pioneers,
Confessor of condemned men and conspirators,

O Satan, pity me in my long misery!

Adoptive father of all those whom in his wrath
The Lord God banished from his paradise on earth,

O Satan, pity me in my long misery!

Prayer

All praise and glory, Satan, be to you on high,
In Heaven where you reigned, and in Hell where you lie
Defeated, dreaming silently! Grant that I may
Repose my weary soul beside your own one day,
Beneath the Tree of Knowledge whose branches shall spread
Like a resurgent Temple over your proud head!

DEATH

CXLIX. — THE LOVERS' DEATH

We shall have beds imbued with subtle scents,
And ottomans as deep as any tomb,
And flow'rs of mystic fragrance redolent
That under fairer skies for us will bloom.

Burning ever more ardent and more bright,
Our hearts will shine like beacons from above,
Each sending forth its pure reflected light
To the twin mirrors of our endless love.

One evening made of rose and mystic blue,
We shall exchange an ultimate adieu,
A last scintilla of this earthly life;

And later an Angelic form will pass,
To faithfully and joyously revive
The dormant embers and the tarnished glass.

CL. — THE DEATH OF THE POOR

It's Death that comforts us, alas! and makes us live;
It is our lifetime's aim, our only hope and friend;
It fills us like an elixir, and seems to give
Us strength to tread the path of life unto the end;

As we traverse the storms, the winters bleak and cold,
Upon our dark horizon it's the radiant beam;
It is the famous inn of which the book once told,
Where we shall sit and eat, and sleep, and idly dream;

An Angel whose magnetic fingers hold the key
That brings the gift of sleep and blissful reverie,
Who makes the bed in which the naked pauper lies;

It is the mystic granary, the promised land,
It is the poor man's purse, his ancient fatherland,
It is the open portal to the unknown Skies!

CLI. — THE DEATH OF ARTISTS

How often must I shake my little bells, and deign
To kiss your lowly brow, pathetic travesty?
To pierce your bull's-eye, target full of mystery,
How many arrows must my quiver give in vain?

We shall consume our souls in many subtle schemes,
And we'll demolish many armatures before
We contemplate the great Creation we adore,
For which we yearn and weep in our most ardent dreams!

Those who have never known the Idol of their soul,
The sculptors who are damned and suffer obloquy,
Who go beating their breast and brow despairingly,

Have but one hope, bizarre and sombre Capitol!
It is that Death, like a new sun above their tomb,
Will make the flowers of their spirit grow and bloom!

CLII. — THE END OF THE DAY

Beneath a pale, depressing light,
Twisting and dancing pointlessly
Goes Life, gaudy and uncontrite.
And so, when Night voluptuously

On the horizon speaks its name,
Assuaging hunger, purging past
Misfortune, sorrow, even shame,
The Poet tells himself: "At last!

My spirit, like my vertebrae,
Ardently yearns for sweet release;
And, shrouded in dark reverie,

I shall lie down to take my ease,
Wrapped in the curtains of your peace,
O comforting obscurity!"

CLIII. — THE DREAM OF A CURIOUS MAN

To Félix Nadar

Do you perchance, like me, feel pleasurable dole,
And do they say of you: "This man's an oddity!"
— I was about to die, and in my fevered soul
Desire mingled with dread, a curious malady,

Anguish and hope, devoid of any factious whim.
The more the sands of time fatally gathered pace,
The more my pain became both comforting and grim;
My heart was being torn from its familiar place.

I was the child who longs to see the spectacle,
Hating the curtain as a needless obstacle...
At last the bitter truth revealed itself to me:

Death had brought no surprise, and dawn's terrible chill
Enveloped me. — What? Is there nothing more to see?
The curtain had gone up and I was waiting still.

CLIV. — THE VOYAGE

To Maxime Du Camp

I

For children who delight in maps and colour plates,
The world is equal only to their appetite.
Bright lights can make it seem such an enormous place!
And yet how small it is, considered with hindsight!

One morning we depart, our ardent minds afire,
Carried on waves that rise and fall rhythmically,
Our hearts beset by rancour and bitter desire,
Cradling infinite thoughts upon a finite sea:

Some of us, glad to flee a country we despise,
Others, the horror of their birthplace, others still,
Astrologers immersed in a strange woman's eyes,
Subjected to the tyranny of perfumed Circe's will.

In order not to be transmuted into swine,
They drink their fill of light from lambent realms of space;
The biting winds, the searing suns that bronze their skin,
Slowly erase the marks left by her vile embrace.

But the true voyagers are those who put to sea
Simply for travel's sake; they press on, hearts aglow;
They never leave the path of their true destiny,
And though they know not why, they always say: Let's go!

Those whose intense desires resemble cumulus,
Who, like a new recruit who dreams about the gun,
Foresee unending pleasures, vast, voluptuous,
The names of which remain unknown to anyone!

II

We imitate, O horror! balls and spinning tops
That, even while we sleep, gyrate and bounce and run,
And Curiosity, cruel Angel, never stops
Tormenting us, like suns that she has whipped and spun.

Strange destiny whose goal is always on the move,
And, being nowhere, can be anywhere, who knows?
Where Man, whose steadfast hope no obstacle can move,
Continues his eternal quest to find repose!

Our soul is like a ship that seeks Icaria;
"Look there!" someone on deck shouts out in disbelief.
While from the mast come cries of great euphoria:
"O joy and happiness!" — Damnation! It's a reef!

Each tiny island that the lookout boy might see
Is taken to be Eldorado, our last dock;
Imagination, spreading out its panoply,
In the cold light of day finds nothing but a rock.

O that poor lover of exotic chimeras!
Should we clap him in irons and cast him to the sea,
That drunken sailor who sees new Americas
Whose mirage makes the oceans flow more bitterly?

So too the aged vagrant, trudging through the mud,
Dreaming, nose in the air, of heavens bathed in light;
His ever-spellbound eye sees a new Capua
In every humble dwelling lit by candlelight.

III

Amazing voyagers! What noble histories
We read in the unfathomed oceans of your eyes!
Open for us the caskets of your memories,
Those wondrous treasures that are made from stars and skies.

We too, with neither steam nor sail, would cross the seas!
To lighten our ennui, where every day's the same,
Paint on the canvas of our hearts your memories
Of all the wonders that the vast horizons frame.

Tell us, what have you seen?

IV

"We have seen many stars
And many waves; we have seen many beaches too;
And despite many blows, of which we bear the scars,
We often felt the weight of boredom, just like you.

The glory of the sun's rays on the violet sea,
The glory of the cities that in the sunset rise,
Ignited in our hearts a strange anxiety
To plunge into the depths of those alluring skies.

Great vistas and great cities, rich in history,
Could never hold for us the mystical allure
Of scenes formed by the clouds, so full of mystery.
And longing always left us anxious and unsure!

— Enjoyment bolsters up and strengthens our desire.
Desire, old tree for whom delight is your manure,
Your bark grows thick and hard, and your branches grow higher,
Striving to reach the sky, drawn by the sun's allure.

Will you grow ever taller, great tree more robust
Than even the cypress? — But from our wanderings
We've saved some sketches for your album, you who must
Indulge your avid yearnings for exotic things!

We've bowed to graven images and effigies;
Fine thrones inset with gems of quality supreme;
Imposing palaces whose fabled luxuries
Would be for any banker a ruinous dream.

Costumes that are inebriation for the eyes;
Women with teeth and nails tinted with subtle stains,
And snake charmers whose skills astonish and surprise."

V

And then, and then what else?

VI

"O simple childlike brains!

We never should forget the most important thing:
Across the entire spectrum of humanity,
We witnessed, without seeking, in our wandering,
The tedious round of sin and immorality:

Woman, base slave, self-loving and contemptuous,
Yet unaware that she's so stupid and so vain;
And man, obsessed by greed, wanton, libidinous,
Slave of the slave and gutter flowing in the drain;

The torturer's delight, the martyr's agony;
The feast seasoned with blood to feed the despot's urge;
The lust for power and the curse of tyranny,
The crowd enamoured of the brutalising scourge;

Many religions that are not unlike our own,
All aiming for the sky; and Saintly Piety,
Like a voluptuary upon a bed of down,
In nails and sackcloth seeking joy and ecstasy;

Drunk on its genius, prattling Humanity,
That's just as crazy now as it's been from the first,
Shouting to God, in its unbridled agony,
'O Master, my own likeness, may you now be cursed!'

And those less stupid, brave friends of Insanity,
Fleeing the servile flock that Fate has herded in,
And seeking refuge in opium's sanctuary!
— Such is the entire globe's eternal bulletin."

VII

Such bitter knowledge that we all draw from our voyage!
The world, monotonous and petty, lets us see,
Today, yesterday and tomorrow, our own image:
An oasis of horror in a desert of ennui!

Should we depart? or stay? If you can't stay, then go;
Stay if you can. One runs, another secretly
Remains to thwart harsh Time, that unrelenting foe!
There are, alas! those who are running constantly,

Like the apostles or the lonely wandering Jew,
To whom nothing avails, neither carriage nor ship,
To flee this vicious combatant; there are a few
Who know how to dispatch him without leaving their crib.

When finally he catches up with us, at least
We shall still foster hope, and shout aloud: Let's go!
Just as in former times we set off for the East,
Eyes fixed on the horizon, and with cheeks aglow

We shall embark upon the Sea of Darkness, where
We'll sail, like a young passenger, in joyful haste.
Do you hear those beguiling, deathlike voices there,
That sing: "This way please, those of you who wish to taste

The perfumed Lotus! This is where we gather in
The wondrous fruits whose flavour every joy transcends.
Come and taste their delights, forever savouring
The magic of an afternoon that never ends!"

In those familiar tones we recognise the spectre;
Our friends, like Pylades, stretch out their arms to us.
"To replenish your heart swim out to your Electra!"
Says she whose knees in former times we used to kiss.

VIII

O Death, old captain, let's cast off! The time has come!
This country holds no joy for us. Come! Let's depart!
Although both sea and sky are bathed in inky gloom,
You know that your bright flame still burns in every heart!

Pour us your poisoned draught, and let its comfort dwell
Within us; let your ardent fire our hearts imbue;
We'll fathom the abyss, be it Heaven or Hell,
To seek out the Unknown, and to find something *new*!

OTHER POEMS

TO THÉODORE DE BANVILLE

So firmly did you grasp the Goddess by her hair
That, judging by your mastery and nonchalance,
You might have been compared, forgive my impudence,
To some young ruffian flooring his mistress there.

With clarity of eye, with such precocity,
You've shown how proud you are to be an architect
Of writings which are so audaciously correct
That in them we foresee your full maturity.

Poet, our blood escapes through every single pore;
Was it merely by chance the robe of the Centaur,
Which to a morbid stream transmuted every vein,

Was three times dipped and tinted by the subtle biles
Of those vindictive, monstrous, hideous reptiles
That in his crib the infant Hercules had slain?

VERSES FOR THE PORTRAIT OF HONORÉ DAUMIER

The man you see depicted here,
Whose art of subtle parody
Instructs us in self-mockery,
Dear reader, truly is a seer.

He is a master of the art
Of satire, but the energy
With which he paints Iniquity
Reveals the beauty of his heart.

When he laughs, it is not the sneer
Of Melmoth or of Mephisto
Beneath the torch of Alecto
Which burns them, but chills us with fear.

Their laugh, alas! of gaiety
Is but a sham, an artifice;
His own, aglow with unfeigned bliss,
Bears witness to his charity.

ON THE DEBUT OF AMINA BOSCHETTI
At the Théatre de la Monnaie in Brussels

Amina leaps, — runs off, — then flutters smilingly;
The Belgian says: "All that is simply Greek to me;
The only woodland nymphs I know, I must declare,
Are those of the *Montagne-aux-Herbes-Potagères.*"

On slender dainty feet, her eyes sparkling with glee,
Amina pours forth floods of wit and ecstasy;
The Belgian says: "Begone, perfidious temptation!
My wife does not afford such light gratification."

You surely do not know, nymph of triumphant stance,
You who would gladly teach an elephant to dance,
Lend laughter to a stork, teach an owl gaiety,

That on such glowing grace the Belgian can but sneer!
And that, if gentle Bacchus poured him burgundy,
The monster would reply: "I'd rather have a beer!"

TO MR EUGÈNE FROMENTIN
concerning a pest who called himself a friend

He told me he was very rich,
But that he feared the cholera;
— That he was careful with his cash
But that he loved the opera;

— That Nature left him much inspired,
Being by Corot ably taught;
— And although not as yet acquired,
A carriage would be shortly bought;

— That he loved marble, slate and brick,
And golden wood of finest grade;
— That in his workshop he possessed
Three craftsmen masters of their trade;

— That he had, not to count the rest,
Twenty thousand shares in the North;
— And that he'd purchased, for a song,
Some picture frames by Oppenord;

— That he'd go even to Luzarches
To find the best of bric-à-brac,
And from the mart of Patriarches
He'd always bring some treasures back;

— That he did not much like his wife
Nor his dear mother, sad to say,
And yet he sought eternal life,
And knew the works of Niboyet!

— That he'd a taste for carnal bliss,
And on a tedious Roman stay
A woman, stricken by phthisis,
Of love for him had passed away.

For fully three hours and a half
That busybody from Tournai
Churned out the story of his life –
I thought my brain would burst that day!

If I tried to describe my pain,
I'd never know quite when to cease;
And, hoping not to go insane,
I thought: "Can't I just have some peace!"

And like one who is ill at ease,
But cannot make good his escape,
I rubbed my bottom on my seat
And dreamed of his impending fate.

That monster, Bastogne is his name,
Was fleeing from the dreaded plague;
I'd flee as far as Gascony,
Or throw myself into the Seine,

If, in this Paris he so fears,
When we have all returned some day,
I should encounter once again
That tiresome native of Tournai.

A LIVELY TAVERN
(on the road from Brussels to Uccle)

You who are fond of skeletons
And other loathsome allegories,
To season your debaucheries
(Were you but vegetarian!)

Old Pharaoh, Monsieur Monselet!
Before this unexpected sign
I thought of you: *Come in and dine,
With Graveyard View, Estaminet!*

LOLA OF VALENCIA

Among the many beauties that everywhere we see,
I am aware, my friends, that fondness fluctuates;
But in Lola we see a jewel that radiates
The unexpected charm of rose and ebony.

ALPHABETICAL INDEX

Abel and Cain 217
Abyss (The) 124
Afternoon Song 103
Albatross (The) 20
Alchemy of Sorrow 135
All of Her 73
Allegory 207
Autumn Song 100
Autumn Sonnet 114
Bad Monk (The) 29
Balcony (The) 67
Beacons (The) 25
Beatrice (The) 208
Beautiful Ship (The) 89
Beauty 39
Benediction 17
Bertha's Eyes 91
Blind (The) 158
Carrion (A) 56
Cask of Hatred (The) 123
Cat (The) *(Come, my dear cat ...)* 65
Cat (The) *(Within my fancy...)* 87
Cats 116
Causerie 99
Clock (The) 144
Confession 80
Congenial Horror 136
Correspondences 22
Cracked Bell (The) 125
Damned Women *(In the pale light...)* 195
Damned Women *(Like contemplative beasts...)* 194
Dancing Serpent (The) 54
Danse Macabre 166
De Profundis Clamavi 60
Death of Artists (The) 227
Death of the Poor (The) 226
Destruction 188

Don Juan in Hell 37
Dream of a Curious Man (The) 229
Duellum 66
Elevation 21
End of the Day (The) 228
Enemy (The) 30
Epigraph for a Condemned Book 13
Epilogue 176
Evening Harmony 83
Evening Twilight 163
Exotic Fragrance 47
Fantastic Engraving (A) 121
Flask (The) 84
Former Life (The) 33
Fountain (The) 92
Fountain of Blood (The) 206
Franciscae Meae Laudes 106
Gaming Table (The) 165
Ghost (The) 113
Giantess (The) 41
Happy Corpse (The) 122
Head of Hair (The) 48
Hymn 74
Hymn to Beauty 46
I offer you these verses so that if my renown... 71
I never shall forget our little cottage there... 169
I love to contemplate those naked days of old... 23
I love you as I love the starlit firmament... 50
Ideal (The) 40
In Praise of My Francesca 107
Invitation to a Journey 94
Irremediable (The) 139
Irreparable (The) 97
Jewels (The) 43
Jinx (The) 32
Labouring Skeleton (The) 161
Laments of an Icarus (The) 132
Landscape 147
Lesbos 191

Lethe (The) 62
Lid (The) 137
Litanies of Satan (The) 219
Little Old Women (The) 155
Lively Tavern (A) 244
Living Torch (The) 76
Lola of Valencia 245
Lonely Man's Wine (The) 183
Love and the Skull 211
Love of Falsehood (The) 168
Lovers' Death (The) 225
Lovers' Wine (The) 184
Man and the Sea 36
Martyr (A) 189
Mask (The) 44
Metamorphoses of the Vampire (The) 203
Midnight Review (The) 143
Mist and Rain 172
Mœsta et Errabunda 112
Monster (The) 199
Morning Twilight 175
Murderer's Wine (The) 181
Music 119
Obsession 133
Offended Moon (The) 171
On the Début of Amina Boschetti 241
One night as I lay with a dreadful Jewish whore... 63
Owls (The) 117
Pagan's Prayer (A) 202
Parisian Dream (A) 173
Phantom (A) 69
Pipe (The) 118
Poison (The) 85
Portender (The) 142
Possessed (The) 68
Posthumous Remorse 64
Promises of a Face (The) 42
Punishment of Pride 38
Rag-Pickers' Wine (The) 180

Ransom (The) 31
Rebel (The) 205
Reversibility 79
Sad Madrigal (A) 58
Saint Peter's Denial 215
Sed Non Satiata 52
Self-Communion 160
Self-Tormented (The) 138
Semper Eadem 72
Sepulchre 120
Seven Old Men (The) 153
Sick Muse (The) 27
Sisina 105
Sorrows of the Moon 115
Soul of Wine (The) 179
Spiritual Dawn 82
Spleen *(I have more memories...)* 127
Spleen *(I'm like a king...)* 128
Spleen *(Pluviose, venting his ire...)* 126
Spleen *(When the low, heavy sky...)* 129
Sun (The) 148
Sunset of Romanticism (The) 187
Swan (The) 151
"Tasso in Prison" by Eugène Delacroix 141
Taste for the Void (A) 134
The servant with a heart of gold... 170
To a Creole Lady 111
To a Madonna 101
To a Passer-By 159
To a Beggar Girl 149
To a Woman of Malabar 110
To Her Who Is Too Gay 77
To Mr Eugène Fromentin 242
To see her undulating, opalescent dress... 53
To the Reader 15
To Théodore de Banville 239
Travelling Gypsies 35
Troubled Sky (A) 86
Two Good Sisters (The) 204

Unforeseen (The) 130
Vampire (The) 61
Venal Muse (The) 28
Verses for the portrait of Honoré Daumier 240
Very far from here 34
Voice (The) 96
Voyage (The) 230
Voyage to Cythera (A) 209
What will you say tonight, poor solitary soul... 75
You'd take the entire universe into your shrine ... 51

Printed in Great Britain
by Amazon